Jesus and Coffee

30 Morning Devotionals to Kick Start Your Day

Tony L. Warrick

D1444805

Sis. Proctor

PRESENTED TO

Bro. Coggins

BY

20 March 2018

DATE

Be Blessed !

Jesus and Coffee

Cover design by Jamar Jones, www.gi-designs.com

Editorial services by Nyesha Sherman and Ashley Warrick

Printed in the United States of America

ISBN-13: 978-1978080690
ISBN-10: 1978080697

Free Bonus!

Simply as a "Thank you" for downloading this book, I would like to offer you a free eBook to help you start living your best life now.

For Instant Access Go To:

http://bit.ly/DecideEbook

In addition, I am inviting you to be a member of my Dream Team! The Dream Team members are the first to know about new book releases, videos and special offers and have access to exclusive content. You will have the chance to provide comments, criticism, and feedback about book ideas, book titles, and book covers. As well, you will enter a drawing to win a few great prizes, such as:

- An opportunity to win an autographed copy of my books
- An opportunity to win a $25 Visa gift card
- An opportunity to win a free vacation for two

Join the Dream Team by going to:

http://bit.ly/DreamTeamNow

Dedication

I dedicate these devotions to the individual who needs to wake up, feel empowered, and receive God's love, mercy, and the power of His Word. While these daily readings are not meant to replace your private time with God, it is my hope that the readings will be a resource to help you understand and realize your true and full potential.

Table of Contents

For this reason I bow my knees before the Father, from whom every family in heaven and on earth is named, that according to the riches of his glory he may grant you to be strengthened with power through his Spirit in your inner being, so that Christ may dwell in your hearts through faith—that you, being rooted and grounded in love, may have strength to comprehend with all the saints what is the breadth and length and height and depth, and to know the love of Christ that surpasses knowledge, that you may be filled with all the fullness of God.

Ephesians 3:14-19

Introduction

Life doesn't start when you open your eyes in the morning,
it starts when you take the first step towards Jesus.
-Dr. Tony Warrick

Have you ever awakened to the beautiful sounds of birds chirping outside your bedroom window? Or, have you ever awakened to the sweet aroma of your favorite breakfast?

Imagine walking into the kitchen after a hot shower, only to see your spouse cooking your favorite: eggs, bacon, and southern style hash browns. You pour yourself a cup of steaming hot coffee as you sit at the table to enjoy your perfect breakfast and catch up on your preferred newsfeed. Your kids are dressed and ready for an exciting day at school.

You jump into the car, go to work, and accomplish everything your boss put on your to-do list. You have a great conversation about your next promotion and, to top things off, your colleagues surprise you with freshly baked Krispy Kreme donuts, just because they love all the hard work you've been doing. You are relaxed and happy because you are having the perfect day.

Lucky you, right?

Then again, maybe that isn't you at all.

Maybe your day began with the loud, sharp sound of a barking dog or the aroma of burnt toast. Perhaps you woke up thinking about how much you hate your job.

After a hot shower, you walk into the kitchen, only to see your spouse has presented you with overcooked eggs, spam, and oatmeal. You pour yourself a lukewarm cup of coffee as you sit at the table to eat your breakfast and catch up on the local news. You notice your 7-year-old son is lying on the floor with his socks soaked in the milk he knocked over while stealing his sister's bowl of Fruit Loops. As for your 5-year-old daughter, well she's still wearing her pajamas and tugging at her hair, which looks like a bird's nest.

You jump into the car only to realize it won't start because you left your headlights on the night before. It looks like you'll be late for work, again. When you get to work, your boss is waiting at your desk ready to eat you alive because of a mistake the mailroom clerk made two weeks ago. A box of donuts would have been nice, but your co-workers really don't like you.

Bad luck, right?

Not really!

If we are completely honest, we have all had our share of both pleasant and horrible mornings. But did you know that your great days and your bad days have little to do with the occasional morning car trouble, your nasty breakfast, your rowdy kids, or your horrible boss? As a matter of fact, they have nothing to do with luck either! Please remember this:

The tone of your day has everything to do with the first hour of your day.

Believe it or not, how you spend the first 60 minutes of your day can have a major influence on your temperament, drive, mental energy, and well-being. This is why some people grab life with enthusiasm and take control of their futures, and some people have trouble breaking out of the "barely getting by" mentality. Actually, most successful people consider the first hour of the day a prime time for self-improvement.

So, let me ask you, what did you do in your first hour today? What was the first thing you thought about? Was it going back to sleep? Your mother's cooking? How about building your business? Your first hour has power!

11

The Hour of Power

Have you ever noticed how disruptions and difficulties have the habit of striking around the same time your enthusiasm, inspiration, and motivation slowly start to fade? I've learned, however, that people who begin their day with productivity can build on that momentum all day long which leads to success. Some of the most dynamic and innovative minds are attacking the most important things first before the demands of the day interfere.

Here are a few of the things I noticed go-getters do before most individuals finish their first cup of coffee:

- Fix their family breakfast because they were told that it is the most important meal of the day.
- Exercise to improve their physical and mental energy.
- Work on their personal goals and projects outside the scope of their job.
- Complete menial tasks so they don't have to worry about them for the rest of the day.

Whatever they elect to do, the secret to a successful day depends on how they spend their first 60 minutes.

Now I have to admit, focusing on the first hour of my day was a tough lesson for me. I was not a morning person. For as long as I can recall, waking up early has never come naturally for me. I remember hating my 8 a.m. classes with a passion when I was in college, because I wasn't one of those individuals who sprang into action early in the day.

When I joined the fire department, I was a "night owl." Instead of sleeping through the night, I would take mini naps in the evening because I enjoyed sleeping through most of the morning after I'd gotten off duty. I had trained myself to be highly productive and creative in the afternoons.

When I became an educator, I woke up at the last possible minute to squeeze in a shower, walk the dog, make some tea, and get to work on time.

However, there was a season in my life, during which I went through a very challenging and demanding time. Life's troubles were gradually wearing me down and I was becoming realistically bitter, hesitant, and backward looking. I recognized that if I did not do something different and regain control, I was going to be like a derailed train coming off the tracks. Then one day, I watched a video about Tony Robbins' *Hour of Power*.

Here is what I learned: If we want to set up a life that is magnificent and push through our toughest limitations, we have to restructure our day. By creating margins in the morning, we can condition our mind, body, and emotions for extraordinary results. I quickly figured out that:

Creating more boundaries in your life will create space for what's significant, and not simply what's crucial.

When our boundaries in life decrease, our stress increases. When you're not hurrying, you have time to think, time to relax, and time to enjoy life. Creating margins in the morning enables greater opportunity! So, I stopped everything I was doing and reviewed my morning routine.

I learned a long time ago that the best way to make changes to anything is to start with the end result in mind. My end result was creating more space between rest and exhaustion, a gap between breathing freely and suffocating from the demands of the day.

Then I wondered, "What would the Christian approach be?"

If successful people are concentrating on their most important concern first, what about making space for our relationship with Jesus in the morning?

Now, please don't get me wrong, I truly believe that exercise, work, and family are significantly important, but our relationship with Jesus is significantly more important.

Starting on a Spiritual Note

Every morning lean your arms awhile

upon the windowsill of Heaven

and gaze upon the Lord.

Then with the vision in your heart,

turn strong to meet your day.

With just a few lines, this lovely but powerful poem by Thomas Blake captured the importance of starting on a spiritual note.

Let me be honest, early morning devotions never crossed my mind, because I had time in my day to read the Bible and spend some time with the Lord. However, once I began the new routine of spending time with God first thing in the morning, my days radically changed. The problems didn't go away, but the negative, anxious, stressful, and fearful thoughts did start to go away. Little by little, when I started my day by filling my mind with God's truth, those old thoughts didn't have a leg to stand on anymore. I was beginning to see my day in a completely new light.

In the first 60 minutes of your day, your thoughts are certainly more expanded, more free-flowing, and more investigational. Therefore, once you have fixed your minds and heart on the Lord, with a rested body, you are able to face the day and whatever it may present. This means, every day with a free-flowing mind, you have an opportunity to meet with God in worship; to thank Him for His love, grace, and goodness. How powerful is that?

Throughout history, the children of God developed a vital habit in life—to make God their first priority. These godly men and women understood:

To break through barriers and move forward in life, the start of your day has to be rooted in the Lord.

The first thing King David did when he awoke was worship God through prayer because he recognized his need for God's assistance. David cried out, *"O Lord, in the morning you hear my voice; in the morning I prepare a sacrifice for you and watch" (Psalm 5:3).*

We can also follow the example of our Lord and Savior, Jesus Christ. Mark reports that even though Jesus was in the midst of an extremely busy schedule, he still took time to communicate with the Heavenly Father before the burdens of the day began. *"And rising very early in the morning, while it was still dark, he departed and went out to a desolate place, and there he prayed" (Mark 1:35).*

Here's the thing, I know God is available to us at any and all times. And the wise and mature followers of Jesus

Christ will seek Him frequently, regardless of the hour of the day or night. Nonetheless, we need to come into the Lord's presence when we are at our best and our best is when we first wake up.

For that reason, it doesn't matter if you are insane like me and wake up at 4 a.m., or sleep until noon. The first 60 minutes of the day are so vital to your productivity because it establishes your attitude for the remainder of the day. Therefore, there is no better way to kick-start your day than with the Lord.

Kick-Start Your Day

Do you believe we are shaped by our thoughts? Do you believe you become what you think? Oprah Winfrey once said, "You don't become what you want, you become what you believe."

Do you agree?

The Bible says in Proverbs 4:23, *"Keep your heart with all vigilance, for from it flows the springs of life."* Let me say it this way:

Stay cautious about how you think; your life is shaped by your thoughts.

I know life can become chaotic and demanding at times, but I've learned that one simple thought can focus your mind and align your heart. Remember, you were created in the image of God, which means your thoughts and your words can create the life you desire.

In other words, if you think godly thoughts and affirm positive words, you can enrich your life; you can free yourself from any emotional trauma. With the help of the Holy Spirit, the power of your thoughts has an incredible ability to shape your life for greatness.

Can you envision on the canvas of your imagination where one positive and godly thought can lead you each day?

It does not have to become a major out-of-bed experience. It's about you and Jesus connecting, fellowshipping together. It's about receiving what God wants to give you each and every day. It's about coming before the Lord seeking wisdom and guidance.

It might be five minutes, fifteen minutes, or the complete hour, but starting your day with Jesus and meditating on His words will allow you to begin your day with the right perspective and encourage you to seek the joy in the midst of every moment and circumstance.

Spending time with Jesus will empower you to pursue your dreams, create change, and bring unconditional love and hope. That is why I created this book.

In this book,

- I believe you will find devotional readings that will recalibrate and position your thoughts every morning for the next 30 days.
- I believe you will find 30 days of empowering thoughts, which can reap a great spiritual harvest and provide an overflow of blessings.
- I believe you will find stories that will help you live in the fullness for which you were created.
- I believe you will find scriptures that will strengthen you in the midst of your challenges.
- I believe you will find 30 prayers that will help you walk boldly before the open door that God has provided for you.

Please understand that your growth is directly related to the time spent in prayer and reading God's Word. The more you study, the deeper the things that God reveals will be.

Therefore, starting tomorrow, get your favorite coffee, latte, espresso, or cappuccino and sit down with Jesus. Open this book and allow Him to love on you, speak to you, and lead you. You will feel empowered when you kick-start your day with Jesus and Coffee.

Day 1

4 Keys to a More Powerful Prayer Life

Call to me and I will answer you, and will tell you great and hidden things that you have not known. ~ Jeremiah 33:3

Disclaimer: There is no way I can write all I want to say about prayer, but I believe the Holy Spirit has commanded me to help you with your prayer life. In order for you to recognize the power of this book's content, we have to talk about prayer on day one. Therefore, today's devotional will be a little longer than normal, but it is extremely important that you understand this Kingdom concept of prayer. So, let's dig in!

From Christians to Jews, to Muslims, to Hindus, to Buddhists, to heathens, nearly the world's complete population does it. Our favorite sports teams do it, our favorite actors do it, even our enemies do it. Almost everyone claims to pray. Yet, many individuals do not understand it. Even those who practice it consistently are frequently unsure about how it works.

Most believers in Jesus Christ do not have a functional understanding of prayer. They are mindful that they are supposed to do it, so they imitate what they've heard and/or seen, regardless of whether they believe it truly works.

However, it is difficult to maximize something you do not understand! Thus, the most logical question would be "What is prayer?"

1. Prayer is our way to communicate with the unseen God.
2. Prayer is agreeing with God's plans and purposes, in order for them to be accomplished on earth.
3. Prayer is man exercising his legal right on earth in order to summon heaven's influence on it.
4. Prayer is the creation getting the Creator involved in any given situation.

Because we are ambassadors of the Kingdom of Heaven, prayer is the most important Kingdom principle on earth and our number one responsibility. In other words, prayer is not an option for a believer in Jesus Christ. It is a necessity.

Here is my definition of prayer:

Prayer is an earthly warrant authorizing Heaven's interference.

Let us take this a step further...

As you already know, our Heavenly Father has sovereign power over all His creations. Nevertheless, He did something that was very interesting in Genesis 1:26 -28. God gave humankind legal authority to rule over the earth. Psalm 115:16 says, *"The heavens are the LORD's heavens, but the earth he has given to the children of man."*

Since the earth was given to mankind, and God honors His agreement with mankind, He works through us when He wants to accomplish things on earth. Our Heavenly Father, who is faithful to His word, was so dedicated to this agreement with humanity that when He wanted to function unrestricted on earth He came as a man Himself, Jesus Christ.

Therefore, prayer is a result of God's faithfulness to His word and His established governmental system between Heaven and earth. Here is something I learned a few years ago:

Without God, we cannot move and without us, God will not move!

Let me be clear, I'm not saying that God cannot, but from what we understand from the Bible, He will not because He chooses to operate on earth with the cooperation of mankind. God is actively seeking the cooperation of a human to agree with His plan and purposes, which will empower our lives and advance the Kingdom of God.

So, what does this mean for you today?

It means that prayer greatly involves knowing the **will** of God, and agreeing with that **will** to come to pass. It means you have the authority to move mountains out of your way through your faith in Jesus Christ. It means you are powerful! It means you are not a victim of your circumstances but you have victory over your circumstances.

Here are four keys to a more powerful prayer life:

1. **Base your requests on God's sovereignty.** Understand that God is the creator and you are the creation. Therefore, pray with the expectation that God will answer you because you are His child and He is a faithful, loving, and magnificent Father.

2. **Confess your sins.** Admit any thought or action that falls short of God's will and/or any transgression against the laws of God.

3. **Claim the promises of God.** If you honor God and claim His promises with a right attitude and pure motives, you will receive what you asked for, according to His will, and you will grow in intimacy with Him.

4. **Be very specific about what you ask for.** If you want specific answers to prayer, then make specific requests. If your prayers contain general appeals, how will you know if they are answered?

Starting right now, after every devotional, you will join me in prayer so we can see Jesus do more than we could ever imagine while experiencing the peace and joy that God freely gives each day.

Cream and Sugar...

- *"Do not be anxious about anything, but in everything by prayer and supplication with thanksgiving let your requests be made known to God."* **Philippians 4:6**
- *"If you abide in me, and my words abide in you, ask whatever you wish, and it will be done for you."* **John 15:7**

Say this Prayer:

Dear Heavenly Father,

Today I want to thank you for the understanding and realization that I have both a right and a responsibility to pray. My right to pray allows me to come confidently before Your throne, and my responsibility to pray puts a burden on me to intercede in those situations that need Your influence. I am rightly re-committing myself to my prayer life. I declare this by faith, in Jesus' name. Amen.

Day 2

It All Begins with a Decision

Therefore choose life, that you and your offspring may live, loving the Lord your God, obeying his voice and holding fast to him, for he is your life and length of days, that you may dwell in the land...~ Deuteronomy 30:19-20

I am so encouraged today for many reasons; one reason in particular is life changing. I truly believe a moment can change your life, but it all begins with a decision. Sounds philosophical but in fact, it is a simple idea to comprehend. I have several quick questions to ask you:

- Why do some individuals have horrible attitudes and others do not?

- Why do some individuals nitpick and complain while others are thankful?

- Why do some individuals live with worry and despair while others live with peace and joy?

- Why do some individuals sabotage their well-being with negativity and others adopt a healthy lifestyle of positivity?

- Why are some individuals riddled with greed and distrust while others pursue greatness, love, faith, and hope?

The answer to all of the above questions is very simple.

26

It is a decision!

None of us can go back and change what we did yesterday, last year, or a decade ago but we can decide to let go of the past and move forward by choosing life. Now, I do not mean to come off rude but your life is the outcome of the decisions you've made. If you do not love your life, it is time to make better decisions.

Good and bad decisions are usually based on how you feel, but godly decisions are based on godly revelations and biblical truths.

The good news is that you can start making better decisions by choosing Jesus. With Jesus as your focus, you can let go of the pain from a loss, you can let go of the frustration of not accomplishing your goals, and you can let go of the sorrow of not becoming more.

With Jesus, you can embrace all you are and all you can be. With Jesus, nothing is hopeless. With Jesus, it is never too late. You cannot change your yesterday, but with Jesus, the decisions you make right now can change your today.

Therefore, anytime you find yourself going back and forth on a decision, take the time to go back to the person you trust with your heart, Jesus. Decide that no matter what the situation may look like, no matter the disappointments that come, you are going to fix your heart on the Word of God.

It all begins with a decision, and if you decide to be great, you will and your dissatisfactions will become the stepping-stones to something better. Yesterday happened, but today is the day to be strong and have courage because the battle is the Lord's, and He is on your side. Fall into His loving arms today; you can trust Him.

Cream and Sugar...

- *"Let me hear Your loving kindness in the morning; For I trust in You; Teach me the way in which I should walk; For to You I lift up my soul."* **Psalm 143:8**
- *"Make me to know your ways, O Lord; teach me your paths. Lead me in your truth and teach me, for you are the God of my salvation; for you I wait all the day long."*

  Psalm 25:4-5

Say this Prayer:

Dear Heavenly Father,

Today I want to thank You for not leaving me without guidance and direction on matters that are difficult for me to figure out. Help me make wise decisions, which will bring You glory and honor. Let my decisions be the reflection of Your love for me. I declare this by faith, in Jesus' name, Amen.

Day 3

What Are You Magnifying?

Oh, magnify the Lord with me, and let us exalt his name together!
~Psalm 34:3

Magnification is the process of enlarging the appearance, but not the physical size of something. In other words, magnification enlarges beyond the truth, giving false or misleading information, which changes our perspective.

For example, everyone knows that a magnifying glass makes things appear larger than they are in reality. Subsequently, when we magnify an object we are able to make new discoveries, which influence our viewpoint.

Did you know that we have a habit of magnifying non-physical things also?

Think about the news stories and headlines you've encountered this week. Is it possible that either your local news station or your local newspaper magnified a story, making it bigger than it was originally? By discussing the story repeatedly, the story becomes larger, influencing your outlook on it.

The more you reflect on something, the larger you perceive it to be. That is why you must have the right perspective about your problems. If you focus on things that did not happen for you or how someone was hateful towards you, those issues can seem so large that they consume you. However, if you focus on Jesus and magnify Him, things will seem simple and you will be consumed by His love and grace.

Do not focus on what is seen, focus on what is unseen. For what is seen is temporary, but what is unseen is eternal.

It is time for you to magnify the great things in your life. I want you to focus on all the amazing things God has done for you. Think about how much Jesus loves you and what He endured for you. Meditate on the goals, promises, and dreams He has given you. Magnify His holy words!

Today, I want to encourage you to keep the right perspective. I would like you to count your blessings by magnifying five awesome things God is doing in your life. Then I want you to hold that list close to your heart and think about how great your God is.

Write your list:

1. _____

2. _____

3. _____

4. _____

5. _____

The gift of today is that Jesus' yoke is easy and His burden is light. When you magnify Him in every area of your life, you embrace the victory He has in store for you! You will start seeing what God sees, feeling what God feels, and hearing what God hears. With Christ's victory in our heart, you cannot help but achieve those promises He has given you.

Cream and Sugar...

- *"You will seek me and find me, when you seek me with all your heart." **Jeremiah 29:13***
- *"Let the words of my mouth and the meditation of my heart be acceptable in your sight, O Lord, my rock and my redeemer." **Psalm 19:14***

Say this Prayer:

Dear Heavenly Father,

Today I want to confess the weakness of my actions to magnify you. Help me not to focus on my circumstances nor the opinions of other people. Let me only be concerned with that which You tell me in your Word. In Jesus name, I pray, Amen.

Day 4

Who Are You?

Before I formed you in the womb I knew you, and before you were born I consecrated you; I appointed you a prophet to the nations. ~Jeremiah 1:5

Who or what are you allowing to determine your identity?

Truth be told, we all have an identity. Many of our identities center on our success, our heritage, our ministries, our gifting or talent, our jobs, our children, our past, and our marital status. We can also find our identities wrapped in some form of trauma, infertility, poverty, and in our failures. However, that is not who we are!

God never wanted you to be defined by somebody else's thoughts. It does not matter if it is your parents, your spouse, your girlfriend or boyfriend, your boss, or even your friends. God created you to be you!

If you are going to be everything God created you to be, you have to stop letting people and situations define who you really are. You must stop allowing individuals to put you into their mold. You have a decision to make:

You can sit around and worry about what someone else thinks of you or you can get in the Word of God and know what God says about you!

I want you to remember today that the greatest potter of all time created you. He had visions about you long before you were born. God is pouring Himself into you, shaping every part of your life into an amazing work of art. Therefore, if you want to be unfazed and undaunted by whatever occurred in your past and the problems of today, you must accept these never-failing truths:

- You are a child of God made in His image.
- You are anointed by God.
- You are victorious through Jesus Christ.
- You are the light of the world.
- You are a member of a chosen race, a royal priesthood, a holy nation.
- You have been given a spirit of power, love, and self-control.
- You have been made righteous.

I would like for you to look in the mirror every day for the next 26 days and repeat the following affirmations about your identity in Jesus Christ.

✓ I have been justified, redeemed, and forgiven by the grace of Jesus Christ.

✓ I have found boldness, wisdom, and righteousness in Jesus Christ.

✓ I have been set free because of God's love and mercy through my faith in Jesus Christ.

✓ I have been created to produce good works for the glory of God.

✓ I have been made complete in Jesus Christ.

I believe if you repeat these affirmations every day for the next four weeks, your thought patterns will change and you will start noticing God opening up opportunities you never knew existed before. The true measure of success in life is being precisely who God created you to be.

Now, believe deep in your core that God is for you and not against you. He desires for you to prosper, be in good health and have a healthy soul. Stop discrediting yourself for everything you are not, and start giving yourself credit for everything you are. Go show the world you can do all things through Christ Jesus.

Cream and Sugar...

- *"So God created man in his own image, in the image of God he created him; male and female he created them."* **Genesis 1:27**

- *"See what kind of love the Father has given to us, that we should be called children of God; and so we are. The reason why the world does not know us is that it did not know him. Beloved, we are God's children now, and what we will be has not yet appeared; but we know that when he appears we shall be like him, because we shall see him as he is."* **1 John 3:1-2**

Say this Prayer:

Dear Heavenly Father,

Today I want to stop finding my identity in anything other than being Your child. No longer will I put my family, my friends, my career, my talents, or my circumstances before You. Please help me keep Your commandments before me in all things. I pray this in Jesus' name, Amen.

Day 5

This Day Forward

Let your eyes look directly forward, and your gaze be straight before you. ~
Proverbs 4:25

Do you have goals that you're trying to reach? Are you pursuing your purpose in life? Are you chasing your dreams? These are all important questions we must ask ourselves. Here is a better question: did you know that God puts dreams in our hearts and writes a purpose over our lives?

Dreams are not simply the thoughts you experience when you are asleep. They are the joyful ideas, images, and goals that burn in your heart, flood your mind, and saturate your soul. Dreams are what you want to do, how you want to do it, and what type of individual you want to become in the process. They are the revelations you want to experience on your journey to fulfillment.

One of the most important lessons I learned was that to achieve your greatest dreams, you have to embrace the loss of social approval from ignorant people. It was in that revelation I noticed that people deal with their dreams in one of three ways:

- They blame others.

- They justify why they did not achieve their dreams.

- Or they decide to do whatever it takes to make their dreams reality.

In other words, do not accept whatever comes your way in life; block all of the outside noise and concentrate on your dream. Put your energy into building your dreams instead of convincing other people.

From this day forward, I want you to make the choice to do something about the dreams God has given you. Your greatness is never by chance, it is the result of God's love, great intention, genuine determination, and smart execution. I would like you to remember this:

Dreams becoming reality is not a matter of chance, but rather a matter of choice.

God gave you a choice to be the best version of yourself. He gave you a choice to be great, and becoming great is achieved by making God number one in your life. Make the choice to have confidence in Jesus and keep His words near your heart. When your dreams are greater than those little excuses, your dreams will become real and success will follow.

Always remember, living forward is having a dream to build something great for God. And if that is your desire, you will find yourself on an amazing journey toward the fulfillment of your dreams. Envision what will be and move forward to a happily ever after story. God is writing your story of victory, today!

Cream and Sugar...

- *"I will instruct you and teach you in the way you should go; I will counsel you with my eye upon you."* **Psalm 32:8**

- *"Yet the righteous holds to his way, and he who has clean hands grows stronger and stronger."* **Job 17:9**

Say this Prayer:

Dear Heavenly Father,

Today starts a new day for me to be all You created me to be. I am so excited to see all the things you have planned for my life. Thank you for covering my mind, and making me stronger, wiser, and fearless. I give the weight of my burdens all to You. I declare this by faith, in Jesus' name, Amen.

Day 6

Stop with all the Excuses

For we must all appear before the judgment seat of Christ, so that each one may receive what is due for what he has done in the body, whether good or evil. ~2 Corinthians 5:10

When I was a teenager, I had the pleasure of meeting Cathy Hughes, an entrepreneur, radio and television personality, and business executive. If I remember the story correctly, she was rejected by more than thirty banks before she found a lender to purchase a radio station. Shortly after purchasing the station, Cathy Hughes fell on hard times, which forced her and her son to give up their apartment and move into the station to make ends meet. However, over time, the station began turning a profit, largely due to the success of her talk show. Today, Radio One owns more than 55 radio stations throughout the country, and in January 2004, Cathy launched TV One, a cable television channel which is now available in over 57 million homes.

Cathy Hughes had so many reasons to start using excuses, which could have led her to quit: numerous banks rejections, a divorce, an eviction, and still having to raise a growing young boy. Through it all, she continued pursuing her dreams to manifest her destiny.

We can think of so many excuses when it is time for us to start thinking about making a change in our lives and aiming for our dreams. *I am too young; I am too old; someone will disapprove; it is too late; I do not have the time or energy; I do not have the money; I do not know how to get started; it is not in my personality; I have children; or, I am going to get hurt.*

We all have wounds. We all have responsibilities. But we cannot let that be an excuse to sit on the sidelines and not pursue our passions and goals. Sometimes in life, we have to play in pain and stop allowing excuses to hang over our head. We have to stop covering up the excuses with our emotions, justifying our position, and allowing ourselves to be stuck in our current situation. Here is my question for you:

How much longer do you want your excuses to have power over your life?

I have encountered times in my own faith walk when people, including my family, thought I was crazy to pursue what I believed God has called me to do; to pursue my dreams of building something great for God to advance the Kingdom of Heaven.

To be honest, there were times I doubted myself, but I understood that doing nothing was a lot worse than doing

41

something. The Holy Spirt taught me a valuable lesson that I am going to share with you:

It does not matter whether people believe you or not, it is your job to live by faith and not by sight. God will handle the rest!

I want you to know that you are not alone. Jesus is with you every step of the way in life no matter how gloomy, how lonely, or how agonizing those steps may be. Always remember that in order to achieve your destiny, you will have to step off the cliff and dive headfirst into a river of faith, knowing that if you have trouble swimming, Jesus is your life jacket.

Cream and Sugar...

- *"Now faith is the assurance of things hoped for, the conviction of things not seen." **Hebrews 11:1***
- *"And Jesus said to him, "Go your way; your faith has made you well." And immediately he recovered his sight and followed him on the way." **Mark 10:52***

Say this Prayer:

Dear Heavenly Father,

Today, I believe you gave me a vision, a dream, a few desires, and I do not want to disrespect You with my excuses. So, help me Lord to fulfill Your purpose for my life. I put my complete trust in You because I know You will never forsake me. In Jesus' name, I pray, Amen.

Day 7

Duty-Bound by Faith

By faith Noah, being warned by God concerning events as yet unseen, in reverent fear constructed an ark for the saving of his household. By this he condemned the world and became an heir of the righteousness that comes by faith. ~Hebrew 11:7

What is Faith?

Fundamentally, "faith" is having the confidence, trust, and assurance that things hoped for will occur according to the will of God. Faith is the foundation, the infrastructure of all that the Christian life means and all that a follower of Jesus hopes for. Faith is peace during times of uncertainty.

Faith is having an encouraging outlook about what you can do and not being concerned about what you cannot do.

Our faith is what pleases God. It is only when we live by faith that we begin to do the extraordinary for ourselves and our family. As a matter of fact, faith is the necessary element for the success of a family. Whether you are a mother, father, brother or sister, your faith can move mountains on behalf of your family.

We often look at our circumstances, our finances, our education, our gifts, or our network to provide security for our

44

family. However, the best way to shelter and safeguard our family is by our faith. In other words, if our families are the treasure, our faith is the treasure chest.

God has selected you to train your family through faith, to observe His way of life, so that He can bless you with the promises He made to you and the generations after you. So, bring the good news of faith to your family.

Your faith can bind up the brokenhearted and declare liberty to those family members feeling captive. Your faith will proclaim the favor of the Lord and will bring comfort to all who mourn. It will be because of your faith that your family will be called righteous and Jesus will be glorified.

As you remain faithful to follow and obey God, He will bring you and your family into a place of pleasure and fulfillment. God is not asking you to walk by sight, He is asking you to walk by faith. Trust Him because His plans are always for your good. Always remember, a praying person can never be defeated! You have power and authority to speak over yourself, your family, your finances and your dreams! Your greatness is coming by faith!

Cream and Sugar...

- *For truly, I say to you, if you have faith like a grain of mustard seed, you will say to this mountain, 'Move from here to there,' and it will move, and nothing will be impossible for you.* **Matthew 17:20**

- *For by grace you have been saved through faith. And this is not your own doing; it is the gift of God, not a result of works, so that no one may boast.* **Ephesians 2:8-9**

Say this Prayer:

Dear Heavenly Father,

Today Lord, I believe! Let my faith be complete and far-reaching. Let it enter my mind, impacting the way I judge divine and human things. Lord, let my faith be joyful and produce harmony in my spirit. I pray this in Jesus' name, Amen.

Day 8

It's a Trap, Don't Fall for It

Casting all your anxieties on him, because he cares for you. ~1 Peter 5:7

Do not get caught in the monkey trap!

Have you ever heard that statement before?

The statement originates from a very simple technique to catch monkeys. Natives from parts of South America, Africa, and Asia would first hollow out a gourd, leaving the opening just large enough for a monkey to slip their hand and arm through. Then they place a delicious treat inside the gourd, add extra weight to it with sand or pebbles, and place the gourd somewhere the monkey will find it.

The unsuspecting monkey, completely unaware of the trap, would smell the delightful treat and reach into the gourd to grab it. The opening, which is just big enough for the monkey's hand, is too small to allow its clenched fist to pass back through. No matter how much the monkey pulls, the monkey cannot withdraw his treat-filled hand.

Unfortunately, the greedy monkey tries to carry off the gourd, but of course, it's weighted down. Therefore, the monkey struggles, cries, screams, yanks, and jerks until it is exhausted and broken-spirited. Consequently, when the natives come back, they find a tired and frustrated monkey caught by his own fist.

Because the monkey was not wise enough to let go of the treat, the natives collect the monkey, and presumably, head back home to have fresh monkey meat cooked in fresh tomato sauce with chili peppers and onions.

It is easy for us to see how foolish it is to keep holding on to something that really does not have any value, but as Christians, we do it all the time. We hold onto past situations that do not serve us well, creating a trap for ourselves. We hold onto mistakes, anger, resentment, pride, embarrassments, and material things that hold no value. We spend our time replaying situations in our mind where someone hurt us, abused us, or disappointed us, all the while giving up the freedom and victory God has in store for us.

If you want God's best for you, you will have to:

Let go of the old and who you used to be, so that you can embrace the new and who God wants you to be.

Leave the past in the past. Do not get trapped because you are not willing to reposition yourself and your thinking. You serve a God that is mighty and strong, and able to do more than we could ever ask or hope. Therefore, open your mind and your hands so you will be free to hold the blessings of God.

Cream and Sugar...

- *"Set your minds on things that are above, not on things that are on earth." **Colossians 3:2***
- *"You keep him in perfect peace whose mind is stayed on you, because he trusts in you." **Isaiah 26:3***

Say this Prayer:

Dear Heavenly Father,

Today I'm making the decision to trust you with my circumstances. I am letting go of all the pain, hurt, and worry, regardless of how things may feel or appear. I'm ready to take the leap of faith because I know that all things work together for the good of those who love You and are called according to Your purpose. Thank you for giving me the victory. In Jesus' name, I pray, Amen.

Day 9

Forgive Yourself!

For whoever lacks these qualities is so nearsighted that he is blind, having forgotten that he was cleansed from his former sins.~ 2 Peter 1:9

I remember walking along the beach behind my wife, on my birthday, and noticing how the sand underneath her feet would shift, leaving her footprints. As we continued to walk the coastline, the crashing waves would consume the shore, wiping away her footprints leaving no evidence of her being there. Then, I thought to myself,

"Isn't that an awesome picture of forgiveness?"

When God forgives us, it is like the ocean, wiping away the footprints of our sins. It does not matter how many times we make a mistake, it does not matter how many times we blow it; God is permanently ready to accept us with open, loving arms and wipe away the error of our ways.

However, for some reason, we like to hold onto the memories of those past sins and we have a difficult time forgiving ourselves. Have you forgiven yourself for all the mistakes you made?

When one of the teachers of the law asked Jesus about which commandment was the most important, Jesus responded,

> *"The most important is, 'Hear, O Israel: The Lord our God, the Lord is one. And you shall love the Lord your God with all your heart and with all your soul and with all your mind and with all your strength.' The second is this: 'You shall love your neighbor as yourself.' There is no other commandment greater than these."* **Mark 12:29-31**

Let us focus on the part that says, "Love your neighbor as yourself." When we look more carefully at what Jesus said, we notice that He said, "Love your neighbor as yourself," not "then yourself." Jesus is calling us to love ourselves to the same degree as loving others.

Many ask, "Isn't that being selfish?" But how can loving yourself be selfish if we are directed by Jesus to do so? By forgiving yourself, you are giving yourself permission to grow and develop. You are allowing Jesus to do a mighty work within you. Truthfully, it is all about balance!

Sometimes the toughest person for you to forgive is the individual you see in the mirror. I understand you have been upset at yourself for past failures and choices. And I even understand there are moments when you feel ashamed and guilty. But realize that the way you feel about yourself is not how God feels about you. Don't let who you were yesterday interfere with who God has called you to become!

Forgive yourself for all the cruel, heartless, and nasty things you have thought about yourself. Remember, you are God's masterpiece!

It is time for you to forgive yourself; it's time for you to let it go. You have come to Jesus and repented; it is time for you to let it go. The pain from last year, it's time for you to let it go. Your past has already taken too much from you; it's time for you to let it go. Stop letting yesterday steal your future; it's time for you to let it go.

By not letting go and not forgiving yourself, you are denying the work Jesus accomplished for you on the cross! If your sins are forgiven, then you need to see yourself separated from your mistakes.

The same standards of kindness and compassion you show to others are what you need to show yourself. Take the failures of your past and turn it into something great. It is time for you to receive God's wonderful bliss and love. Put your energy towards bettering your life and starting something new. You will experience the breakthrough when you take a step of faith, when you embrace His love, and when you forgive yourself!

Cream and Sugar...

- *"For I will be merciful toward their iniquities, and I will remember their sins no more."* **Hebrews 8:12**
- *"Remember your mercy, O Lord, and your steadfast love, for they have been from of old. Remember not the sins of my youth or my transgressions; according to your steadfast love remember me, for the sake of your goodness, O Lord!"* **Psalm 25:6-7**

Say this Prayer:

Dear Heavenly Father,

Today I understand that there is nothing to gain by not forgiving myself. I want to move forward and fulfill my purpose in life. Because Jesus died for my sins, I have decided to no longer be angry with myself. Thank you for loving me and for Your grace. I pray this in Jesus' name, Amen.

Day 10

The Art of Forgetting

Brothers, I do not consider that I have made it my own. But one thing I do: forgetting what lies behind and straining forward to what lies ahead, I press on toward the goal for the prize of the upward call of God in Christ Jesus. ~Philippians 3:13-14

As you saw from yesterday's reading, we must show the same level of forgiveness to ourselves as we show to others. It is extremely important for us to forgive ourselves from our past sins. But it is equally important for us to forget the burdens of those past sins by letting go of the memories of those burdens.

Our memory is like a two-sided coin: a side of blessings and a side of burden. My older brother was killed in 1996, but I will never forget his genuine smile and his love for life, family, and God. At the same time, I used to be tormented by the memory of his death. I wanted his killer's family to feel the same pain that I was experiencing.

I thank God every day for teaching me how to forgive!

If you are anything like me, there are times when you are plagued by hurtful memories and the hardest part of forgiving is forgetting.

Forgetting is a solo fight. Forgetting requires you to reflect properly, which means your complete focus must be on Jesus and not on memories of yesterday's problems and misery. I am not saying you should reject the hurts you have had. That is psychologically unhealthy. I am implying that forgetting is being intentional about growth, which means evaluating things that have happened in the past, both good and bad, as a means of self-development and growth.

Let's dig a little deeper!

We are told by the world that to experience healing from past difficulties we must explore hurtful things that happened. Similarly, the Word of God teaches us that it can be helpful to reflect on what happened to us in the past in order to understand where we are in the present and how we need to grow and develop for the future.

For example, we should not drive a vehicle by looking in the rearview mirror. The proper way to drive is looking ahead, out of the windshield, and occasionally glancing in the rearview mirror. The goal is to use the information in the mirror to make a good decision on how to continue to drive forward safely. Once we have made a decision on how we are moving forward, we slowly start to forget the memory in the rearview mirror.

In the same way, we need to take periodic glances at yesterday's memories in order to make godly decisions to move forward with our lives. And once we begin to move forward we need to slowly forget the memories of yesterday.

Did you know that intentionally recalling certain memories can lead to forgetting other experiences?

People can conquer certain memories by focusing on more desirable ones. Simply recalling a particular memory repeatedly, like a memory of God's faithfulness, can drive other memories to the back of your mind, resulting in a form of adaptive forgetting.

This is important because God wants you to stop watching reruns of your wrongs and replay His awesome acts. God wants you to forget so you can be alert to what He is about to do in your life today. God wants you to:

Forget the worries and the drama of yesterday's stories and replace them with stories of His mercy and grace.

God is about to provide a river in your wilderness season. God is about to carve out a path through the pounding waves of despair. It is time for you to laugh insanely, live truly, and create beautiful stories for today.

You have one life. One legacy. Make the most of it. When you learn the art of forgetting, God's grace is going to take you from glory to glory, all for His glory.

Cream and Sugar...

- *"The memory of the righteous is a blessing, but the name of the wicked will rot."* **Proverbs 10:7**
- *"But the Helper, the Holy Spirit, whom the Father will send in my name, he will teach you all things and bring to your remembrance all that I have said to you."* **John 14:26**

Say This Prayer:

Dear Heavenly Father,

Today please give me the grace to forget the injustices and mistakes of my past. I choose today to totally focus on You and move into a place of healing. In Jesus' name, I pray, Amen.

Day 11

Jesus Will Be There for You

He leads me beside quiet waters. ~Psalm 23:2

There is one thing I am certain is true: we all have to live in the reality of the unexpected. None of us truly knows what tomorrow promises, what today may produce, what new challenges or new opportunities might appear.

- Do you know anyone who went to the doctor's office when they were not feeling well, only to learn they have cancer invading their body?
- Do you know anyone who went to work on a Friday, only to find out that they have been fired from their job?
- Do you know anyone whose child was killed by the local police?

Life is filled with so many uncertainties. So how do we kick-start our day with assurance and confidence? For those individuals who are followers of Jesus Christ, the answer is by FAITH.

Faith means being sure about the things we hope for and knowing that something is real, even if we do not see it. In other words, when you come across an unforeseen situation,

58

do not panic. Jesus will be there for you. Close your eyes, take a deep breath, and have faith that the Holy Spirit will provide the solution, giving you wisdom in the time of your uncertainty.

Today, I want you to be strong and courageous. Walk with confidence because God's mercies will never end; they are new every morning. When you least expect it, by faith, doors will open, and by faith, your breakthrough will come. Everything you have waited for will be here. Therefore, abide in and abandon yourself in God's faithfulness!

Do not be afraid, for the Lord your God is with you wherever you go. He promises to be a lamp for your feet. If you live by faith and not by sight, I promise everything will be all right. If you fear the present, look back and see how God took care of you in the past. In fact,

People may do you wrong, but God will be your defender. Situations may look impossible, but the impossible is very possible with God.

God will never turn His heart away from you! He is closer to you than you think. Always remember, God's plan is the master plan and you can cast your cares upon Him for He is good and His love is faithful!

Cream and Sugar...

- *"And whatever you ask in prayer, you will receive, if you have faith."* **Matthew 21:22**
- *"And without faith it is impossible to please him, for whoever would draw near to God must believe that he exists and that he rewards those who seek him."* **Hebrews 11:6**

Say this Prayer:

Dear Heavenly Father,

Today I begin a brand new day. Please help me hold my head up high and walk forward with confidence. You are a faithful God who will certainly walk with me every step of the way. Empower me by the Holy Spirit to follow Your ways. I pray this in Jesus' name, Amen.

Day 12

You Were Wonderfully Made

For you formed my inward parts; you knitted me together in my mother's womb. I praise you, for I am fearfully and wonderfully made. Wonderful are your works; my soul knows it very well. ~Psalm 139: 13-14

Have you ever heard the story about the lonely goat sitting in the zoo? If you cannot remember, let me jog your memory.

All day long, people would walk by the cages looking at all the animals. However, no one would ever stop in front of the lonely goat's cage. No one would ever show him any attention or interest.

Early one Saturday morning, a little kid named Timmy strolled by the goat's cage. He stopped, with a lollipop in his hand, and asked the goat, "Where are the tigers, Mr. Goat?" The goat stood in a rigid position with his chin directly forward and began to belch out a great roar. The goat transformed himself into a tiger.

Unfortunately, Timmy's love for tigers changed after a couple of minutes. When the goat noticed, it began to quack like a duck. When Timmy said, "You are too small!" The goat started trumpeting like an elephant, but Timmy went in search of flamingoes.

The goat was upset and depressed, and feeling lost and rejected. The goat thought to himself, "While trying to find someone to love me, I have changed so many times. Oh, how I wish I had remained a goat and waited for a goat lover."

So many people are at war with themselves, and like the goat, they are trying to change who they are and the way they look to please someone else.

The goat learned a valuable lesson. After all the changes, the goat still could not make Timmy happy nor receive the love it was looking for. The Bible says in Psalms 139:14, *"we are wonderfully made."* That means you are unique and one-of-a-kind. God took the time to mold you exactly the way He wanted. Every hair on your head, wrinkle on your face, the color of your skin and the color of your eyes was designed this way for a reason.

Today, I want you to know that you are God's beautiful masterpiece. You are God's unique vessel! Your gifts and abilities were given to you for a purpose. You have been designed with an amount of uniqueness to serve a purpose that you can fulfill only by being your unique self.

God has placed a mark of excellence upon you! You are not ordinary; you are extraordinary.

It is important for you to stop worrying about what others think about you. Stop discrediting yourself for everything you are not, and start giving yourself credit for everything you are. Stop denying your talents and gifts in fear of criticism and disapproval. Never compromise standards or trade your uniqueness for temporary validation and recognition.

If you are going to be all God created you to be, you have to start by being okay with who you are today and understanding that you will get better. Now, go shine and be amazing! And always remember, God's fingerprints are all over you. YOU are important. YOU have value. YOU are destined for greatness. YOU were wonderfully made!

Cream and Sugar...

- *"The Spirit of God has made me, and the breath of the Almighty gives me life."* **Job 33:4**
- *"For we are his workmanship, created in Christ Jesus for good works, which God prepared beforehand, that we should walk in them."* **Ephesians 2:10**

Say this Prayer:

Dear Heavenly Father,

Today, thank you for helping me realize I'm not here by accident. I realize that you are the cornerstone of my life. I know that what You gave me does not make me timid, but gives me power, love and self-discipline. I love You and want to glorify Your name. I pray this in Jesus' name, Amen.

Day 13

Two Words You Must Embrace

When he was reviled, he did not revile in return; when he suffered, he did not threaten, but continued entrusting himself to him who judges justly.
~ 1 Peter 2:23

I would like to share a thought with you today that comes from more than twenty years of working with people in my community.

Did you know that it is often our mentality which is most profound? Do you want to know the difference between the mentality of a victor and the mentality of a loser? It is having the ability to move forward after a hardship.

We all had times when individuals or situations influenced our lives in a horrible way, and times when we felt cheated, neglected, deeply offended, or abandoned. Perhaps you were facing a difficulty yesterday and you just did not know how to handle it. Whatever the circumstance , your ability to move forward after the situation will help decide whether you thrive or miss the mark. Let us look at the life of Jesus for a powerful example for us to follow.

Our Savior, our Wonderful Counselor, the Prince of Peace, the King of kings, and the Lord of lords came to earth with all power and authority. Yet, people taunted Him, mocked Him, mistreated Him, and lied on Him. Nevertheless, Jesus never tried to defend Himself. He did not get into an argument explaining His position.

Jesus rested in who He was. He rested in His purpose. He rested upon the calling on His life. Jesus was able to move forward because He knew He would have victory in the end.

The way to keep from feeling like a failure and feeling like you cannot win in life is to allow God to develop your character. If you want God to build your character, you have to learn how to deal with the difficulties and disappointments of life by trusting and having faith in God. And know, just like Jesus, that you will have victory in the end.

Romans 5:3-5 says, *"Not only that, but we rejoice in our sufferings, knowing that suffering produces endurance, and endurance produces character, and character produces hope, and hope does not put us to shame, because God's love has been poured into our hearts through the Holy Spirit who has been given to us."*

With that being said, here are two tiny, but valuable words that you must learn to embrace:

Move...Forward.

I want to challenge you to write those words on a *Post-it* note and stick it on the mirror in your bathroom, on the dashboard of your car, and on the computer monitor at your job. Rather than thinking about the lack of fairness in your mind, turn those thoughts loose and move forward.

When you wake up everyday, choose to set your life on a pathway to victory by keeping your eyes straight ahead and ignoring the distractions. Look for opportunities to be humble, and let God advance you to a higher place in His time. Know that your God plans to take care of you, not to abandon you, and plans to give you hope and a fruitful future.

Follow Jesus' example to not seek revenge. Find confidence in knowing who you are in Jesus Christ and let God take care of those individuals who have mistreated you. He will do a much better job than you can anyway! Write this down and meditate on this today:

Move forward to win! For yourself, for your family, for your friends, but mostly, move forward to bring God glory!
Cream and Sugar...

- *"Not that I have already obtained this or am already perfect, but I press on to make it my own, because Christ Jesus has made me his own."* ***Philippians 3:12***

- *"Therefore, since we are surrounded by so great a cloud of witnesses, let us also lay aside every weight, and sin which clings so closely, and let us run with endurance the race that is set before us,"* **Hebrews 12:1**

Say This Prayer:

Dear Heavenly Father,

Today, I ask that You endow me with the gift of perseverance and the courage to endure. Help me to move beyond my sufferings and receive healing from You. Regardless of the pain, please teach me to live those two words...move forward. In Jesus name, I pray, Amen.

Day 14

Fix Your Attitude

Put off your old self, which belongs to your former manner of life and is corrupt through deceitful desires, and to be renewed in the spirit of your minds. ~ Ephesians 4:22 -23

I normally start the first day of class asking my students the fundamental question, "What kind of attitude did you bring to school this year?" Every year, this question brings puzzled looks from everyone.

I am amazed that people normally do not have a high level of attitude awareness compared to physical awareness. Think about it:

- We know when we have stomach pain; we cannot see it, but we can certainly feel it.
- We know when we have headache pain; we cannot see it, but we can certainly feel it.
- We know when we have back pain; we cannot see it, but we can certainly feel it.

So why is it that we do not know when we have a bad attitude? We cannot see it, but we can certainly feel it, and others can feel it also.

Let's be honest, encountering someone with a positive and jolly attitude is a rare occurrence these days, and if you are working in an industry that brings you into close contact with people, you are deeply aware of the highs and lows of other people's attitudes. You notice their facial expressions, their hypocritical smile, or a harsh and faithless remark.

As a Christian, you need to safeguard your attitude while being bold and courageous. Realize that your attitude is a choice. It is a choice that manages the way you perceive the world and the way the world perceives you. Always remember:

A bad attitude can block love and blessings, and stops you from discovering your purpose. Do not be the reason you do not succeed.

I want to encourage you to find the determination, the perseverance, and the tenacity to have a positive attitude. I know you have faced some difficulties and have had several obstacles that seem impossible to overcome, but focus on the promises of God and smile. Jesus has already overcome the world and promised you victory. It is time for you to have a victorious attitude!

When you wake up and start your day tomorrow, you should have an attitude of gratefulness, an attitude of hope, an attitude of love. You should have an attitude of faith, with expectancy, that you will receive every blessing God has in store for you.

The right attitude will keep you going and add fuel to a burning passion. When you have the right attitude, no barrier is too high and no valley too deep. When you fix your attitude, you will start to understand that no dream is too extreme and no challenge is too great.

Cream and Sugar...

- *"Do all things without grumbling or questioning, that you may be blameless and innocent, children of God without blemish in the midst of a crooked and twisted generation, among whom you shine as lights in the world,"* **Philippians 2:14-15**

- *"Finally, brothers, whatever is true, whatever is honorable, whatever is just, whatever is pure, whatever is lovely, whatever is commendable, if there is any excellence, if there is anything worthy of praise, think about these things."* **Philippians 4:8-9**

Say This Prayer:

Dear Heavenly Father,

Today, I make the volitional choice to represent you well through my attitude! Remind me, dear Lord, to also express my appreciation and thanks to those you have placed in my life. Thank you for the generous blessings. In Jesus' name, I pray, Amen.

Day 15

Yes Lord, Use Me!

Now to him who is able to do far more abundantly than all that we ask or think, according to the power at work within us, ~ Ephesians 3:20

Not long ago, a woman reached out to me on Twitter and asked for prayer. Then she followed her request by asking me if I thought God could use her regardless of her past. I found her question very interesting and I pondered, "How many other Christians wonder if God can use them?"

Have you ever asked yourself, "Can God really use my life?"

If you are anything like me, when you fell in love with Jesus Christ, you had a profound desire for Him to use you for His glory. Often, our feeling of inadequacy challenges our deep desire to be used, and every now and then, the guilt over past actions fuels our lack of self-assurance. However, I want you to know that God will use you if you are willing to be used, regardless of whether or not you think you are qualified.

In the Bible, we see God using ordinary people to accomplish extraordinary achievements for His glory. People like David, an ordinary shepherd and musician who had an extraordinary calling to slay an extraordinary giant. Or Gideon, an ordinary military leader who had an extraordinary calling to lead a decisive victory over an extraordinary Midianite army despite a massive numerical disadvantage. Think about Mary, an ordinary virgin who had an extraordinary calling to have an extraordinary birth of the Son of God.

Remember the story of Balaam (Numbers 22:28)? Do you remember how God spoke through a donkey? If God can use a donkey, He definitely can use you because **YOU ARE NOT ORDINARY!**

When God becomes Lord over someone's life, they go from ordinary to extraordinary. In addition to that, you have an extraordinary calling on your life.

God is looking to birth and fulfill people's hopes and dreams. He is looking for individuals who are totally committed to Him and are willing to be used by Him for His purpose.

Here is my question for you: Do you believe that God can do extraordinary things, impossible things, through your life?

The Apostle Paul did. He prayed: *"Now to him who is able to do far more abundantly than all that we ask or think, according to the power at work within us, to him be glory in the church and in Christ Jesus throughout all generations, forever and ever. Amen." (Ephesians 3:20-21)*

So, what has God called you to do? Let me tell you. It is something magnificent, amazing, and extraordinary! All you have to do is say, "Yes Lord, use me!" You do not have to have it all together. Not everything has to make sense.

Do not get trapped by the paralysis of analysis!

If you wait for everything to align perfectly, you will never be the person God created you to be. God is not looking for your ability as much as he wants your availability. God wants your faithfulness and willingness to say, "Yes Lord, use me!"

Cream and Sugar...

- *"As each has received a gift, use it to serve one another, as good stewards of God's varied grace:"* **1 Peter 4:10**
- *"A man's gift makes room for him and brings him before the great."* **Proverbs 18:16**

Say this Prayer:

Dear Heavenly Father,

Today, I do thank You for making Yourself real to me. Help me not to limit my service to You because of a sense of inadequacy. Remind me that I can do whatever you call me to do; for you have promised to be with me. Give me the strength to use my life in service to you. I pray this, in Jesus' name, Amen.

Day 16

Do You Really Trust Him?

Trust in the Lord with all your heart, and do not lean on your own understanding. In all your ways acknowledge him, and he will make straight your paths. ~Proverbs 3:5-6

When was the last time you received $2,760 dollars for doing nothing? For me, it was about five years ago when there were four checks totaling that exact amount just sitting in my P.O Box.

The checks were a part of a class-action lawsuit that a particular bank agreed to pay former members to avoid the expense and uncertainty of ongoing litigation. This was money that I did not know existed; I had no clue it was being sent to me. Can you imagine how thrilled I was?

I started jumping with excitement! I started dancing right there in the post office. Receiving unexpected money can feel like you've gotten "free money" that you can spend however you like. Well, at least I thought I could spend it however I liked.

God wanted to teach me a lesson about trust. The next day during my prayer time, I heard God ask me to give the money away.

"Lord that is hard for me," I replied. "I need to pay this month's tuition for school."

Four days later, I heard God ask me, "Do you trust me? Give the money away!"

With disappointment in my heart, I submitted to God's will and gave all the money to my local church.

About two weeks later, when it was time to pay my tuition, I received a phone call from the financial-aid office at the college. They were calling to notify me of a scholarship I had been awarded that would pay the remainder of my tuition for that school year. Immediately, I heard God say to my spirit, "Trust in the Lord with all your heart, and lean not on your own understanding."

I learned a valuable lesson that day: no matter what happens, trust in the Lord. Jobs will come and go. Bank accounts will rise and fall. Economies will increase and they will collapse, but it does not matter! We must trust God for our security.

Is there something you are holding onto today that is keeping you from God's best? Today, I want you to put your complete trust in the Lord and let go of what is holding you back. Let go of the pain, anxiety, anger, hurt and bitterness, and Jesus will exchange it for peace, strength, wisdom, favor, and much more. Our Lord and Savior will give you exactly what you need.

Please think about this:

If Jesus Christ can raise up the dead, just imagine what He can do for your life. Trust in Him!

I believe Jesus is a mountain mover. In addition, He has given you the authority to move every mountain out of your life. As a matter of fact, I declare that every mountain and stronghold that is delaying your dreams are presently being removed!

However, you cannot forget to do your part. You have to learn to trust God and be open to seeing things from a new perspective. You have to know that all things work together for your good. Always remember, as God is glorified, His people benefit.

Therefore, trust His process.

Life is a journey of faith, and within the journey, there will be detours, but God is your shepherd, moving you closer to your destination. So, trust your God, trust His process, and know it is a part of His plan Your test will be your testimony.

Cream and Sugar...

- *"When I am afraid, I put my trust in you. In God, whose word I praise, in God I trust; I shall not be afraid. What can flesh do to me?"* **Psalm 56:3-4**

- *"Commit your way to the Lord; trust in him, and he will act."* **Psalm 37:5**

Say this Prayer:

Dear Heavenly Father,

Today, I want to thank You for being my God; the God of the impossible. You can do anything and everything. I will put all my trust in Your ability and not my own. Help me and teach me how to see the problems in my life from Your perspective. You are mighty, powerful, blameless and true. In Jesus' name, Amen.

Day 17

Learning to Say 'No'

Let what you say be simply 'Yes' or 'No'; anything more than this comes from evil. ~Matthew 5:37

"How do you do it?" I asked.

She replied, "Do what?"

"How do you put your foot down sometimes and say no?"

"I just had to learn to say no," she answered. "I used to feel so guilty when I said no, but I had to learn to be true to myself."

This was the start of a conversation between my co-worker, Ms. Delayna Anderson, and I. We were discussing the difficulties of saying "no" to people, especially to individuals we love. We both agreed that saying "no" could seem uncaring and somewhat selfish. We also confessed that a small amount of fear exists in letting other people down. Moreover, there is a fear of being ostracized or criticized, or of jeopardizing a friendship. Then Delayna said something I thought was brilliant.

She said,

"Learning to say no can earn you respect from yourself as well those around you."

"WOW!" I thought. "She is right!"

When I think about it, the ability to say no is carefully linked to self-confidence. When I had low self-assurance and low self-regard, I frequently felt anxious about upsetting others and I had a habit of ranking other people's needs more highly than mine. I would feel drained, worried and irritable because I was undermining any efforts to improve my quality of life.

As Christians, there are times when we find it difficult to say no. Many of us feel compelled to agree with most requests because we are people-pleasers. However, did you know that being a people-pleaser is a form of idolatry?

The Apostle Paul teaches us in Galatians 1:10 that we should not try to win the approval of people, but of God. If pleasing people is the goal, then we must question whether we are serving Christ. Let me say it this way: when you are a people-pleaser, you have allowed people's opinions and thoughts about you to become first in your life, anything you put before God becomes a god. But, if you focus on pleasing Jesus, everything else will fall into place.

I want to start the day by helping you say no, just in case you need to say it today. So, here are five tips for saying no:

1. **Keep your response simple.** If you want to say no, be strong and unwavering, but you do not have to be rude. Use expressions such as "Thanks, but I'm afraid it's not convenient right now." Or, "I'm sorry but I can't help today."

2. **Give yourself some time.** Use expressions like "I'll get back to you later" and then contemplate your options. This tip will give you more confidence to say no.

3. **Consider a compromise**. Suggest ways to move forward that help both of you, but do not compromise if you really want to say no.

4. **Separate refusal from rejection**. It is important for you to remember you are turning down a request, not an individual.

5. **Be true to yourself.** Be clear and honest with yourself about what you truly want. Get to know yourself better and examine what you really want from life.

I want to encourage you today to stop worrying about the way people feel or think about you. Focus on what God wants you to do and leave the consequences to Him. When you learn to say "no" confidently, you will be able to say "yes" faithfully. By the way, many times what God tells you to do is not going to make any sense to the people around you, and it's not supposed to. You have God's approval, and that is all you really need!

Cream and Sugar...

- *"For am I now seeking the approval of man, or of God? Or am I trying to please man? If I were still trying to please man, I would not be a servant of Christ."* **Galatians 1:10**
- *"Whatever you do, work heartily, as for the Lord and not for men,"* **Colossians 3:23**

Say this prayer:

Dear Heavenly Father,

Today, I pray that the thoughts and opinions of others do not distract me. Lord, You know that in my heart I want everyone to be happy, but help me to not put anyone's happiness before You. Please give me the strength to be my honest and authentic self, and guide me by Your Spirit every step of the day. In Jesus' name, I pray, Amen.

Day 18

Forgive Me, Oh God

Let it be known to you therefore, brothers, that through this man

forgiveness of sins is proclaimed to you,

~ Acts 13:38

As Christians, it's safe to say that God plays a significant role in our lives. We worship God with our praise, we worship God with our prayers, we worship God by studying His words, and we even worship God with our money. There is no doubt we do our very best to live productive and godly lives as devoted followers of Jesus Christ. Still, we will never be perfect.

No matter how much we worship God, perfection will always escape us. In fact, as long as we are on this earth, we are going to make mistakes; we will always struggle against temptation and sin. That is one reason Jesus taught His disciples to pray, *"Forgive us our sins … And lead us not into temptation, but deliver us from the evil"* (Matthew 6:13).

God is loving and merciful, and is ready to forgive us of our sins and mistakes! The Bible repeatedly shows us in the New Testament that our Heavenly Father will forgive all of our sins through Jesus Christ. Let's take a look at one of those scriptures.

> *"For all have sinned and fall short of the glory of God, and are justified by his grace as a gift, through the redemption that is in Christ Jesus, whom God put forward as a propitiation by his blood, to be received by faith. This was to show God's righteousness, because in his divine forbearance he had passed over former sins. It was to show his righteousness at the present time, so that he might be just and the justifier of the one who has faith in Jesus." (Romans 3:23-26)*

You should never be shackled to your past because:

God has forgiven you, so you can focus on the present and become everything you were created to be.

Although, God is eager to forgive the sins of His children, simply asking is not enough. There are several important steps that you must take. Here is a roadmap to God's forgiveness:

Step 1. Acknowledge Your Sins

"Have mercy on me, O God, according to your unfailing love; according to your great compassion blot out my transgressions." – Psalms 51:1

Step 2. Confess to God

"Then I acknowledged my sin to you and did not cover up my iniquity. I said, "I will confess my transgressions to the Lord." And you forgave the guilt of my sin." – Psalm 32:5

Step 3. Ask God for Forgiveness

"If my people, who are called by my name, will humble themselves and pray and seek my face and turn from their wicked ways, then I will hear from heaven, and I will forgive their sin and will heal their land." – 2 Chronicles 7:14

Step 4. Change Your Behavior

"Repent, then, and turn to God, so that your sins may be wiped out, that times of refreshing may come from the Lord." – Acts 3:19

Step 5. Seek Forgiveness from Others

"If you forgive those who sin against you, your heavenly Father will forgive you. But if you refuse to forgive others, your Father will not forgive your sins." – Matthew 6:14-15

As long as you are pure and honest in your dedication to move beyond your mistakes and sins, God will forgive you for your transgressions and help you to lead a better life in His image. Always remember, the price has been paid and you do not have to live guilty and condemned. You are receiving forgiveness, by faith, through the love, grace, and mercy of Jesus Christ.

Cream and Sugar...

- *"If we confess our sins, he is faithful and just to forgive us our sins and to cleanse us from all unrighteousness."*
  1 John 1:9
- *"I, I am he who blots out your transgressions for my own sake, and I will not remember your sins."*
  Isaiah 43:25

Say this prayer:

Dear Heavenly Father,

Today it has become clear to me that I have sinned against You and am deserving of punishment. But I am so thankful that Jesus Christ took the punishment that I deserve so that through faith in Him I could be forgiven. I place my trust in You for salvation. Thank You for Your wonderful grace and forgiveness! In Jesus' name, I pray, Amen!

Day 19

God Is Preparing You for Great Things

Behold, I am doing a new thing; now it springs forth, do you not perceive it? I will make a way in the wilderness and rivers in the desert. ~Isaiah 43:19

From the time she was a little girl, everyone counted Wilma out. She was a sickly child who was afflicted with double pneumonia, scarlet fever, and polio and had to wear a brace on her left leg. At the age of nine, this little girl removed the leg brace and she took the steps the doctors told her she would never take. After four years, she developed a graceful stride, which was considered a medical wonder.

Years later, the once sickly young child, who overcame her disabilities with faith, persistence, courage and an unconquerable spirit, became the first American woman to win three gold medals in track and field at the Olympics. She was once quoted saying, "The triumph can't be had without the struggle."

This amazing woman, Wilma Rudolph, was inducted into the U.S. Olympic Hall of Fame and established a foundation to promote amateur athletics. She was able to live an amazing life because her attitude of faith never let her challenges determine her future.

If you are in the midst of a storm, among the thickets and thorns of life and experiencing opposition, please understand that God is preparing you and refining you for greatness. Like Wilma Rudolph, God is developing your faith, persistence, courage, and unconquerable spirit. God loves you too much to promote you before you are ready. Therefore, lean in, trust the loving hand of your Lord, and know that He will lead you to new heights.

Today, I want you to know that God is not preparing the dream for you; He is preparing you for the dream so it can become reality. He is raising you up like a strong tower to shine brightly for the world to see! It is important for you to understand:

When you receive a God-given dream, not a wish or a fantasy, God will give you the strength and courage to make it happen.

You were created to win; you were fashioned to overcome the challenges; you were born to be a champion. So, keep an attitude of faith because what seems impossible to accomplish is very possible with Jesus in your life.

Cream and Sugar...

- *"For the Lord your God is he who goes with you to fight for you against your enemies, to give you the victory."* **Deuteronomy 20:4**

- *"I have said these things to you, that in me you may have peace. In the world you will have tribulation. But take heart; I have overcome the world."* **John 16:33**

Say this Prayer:

Dear Heavenly Father,

Today I ask You to help me become bold as I go throughout this day. When I am tempted to surrender, help me to carry on. Grant me a joyful spirit when things do not go my way. And give me the courage to do whatever needs to be done to bring You glory. I pray this in Jesus' name, Amen.

Day 20

Fear Not!

Fear not, for I am with you; be not dismayed, for I am your God; I will strengthen you, I will help you, I will uphold you with my righteous right hand ~Isaiah 41:10

The state of our world has caused unbelievable concern and fear to permeate the hearts of many. Almost every day on Twitter, I speak with someone who is afraid or anxious about something. I started to wonder at what age do people begin to become afraid. Thus, I proceeded to ask several of my middle school students about fear and I received several different answers.

There was one student I was mentoring and when I asked him, "What are you afraid of?" He answered with a commanding tone in his voice, "Nothing, I'm not scared of anything and I never will be!"

Do you believe he was telling me the truth? If I am completely honest, I believe the majority of us are scared of something or someone. In fact, there are literally hundreds of different phobias.

There are specific phobias, which focus on one fear such as the fear of flying. There are social phobias like the fear of embarrassment or humiliation. And then there's Agoraphobia—the mother of all phobias. This complex phobia is characterized by signs of anxiety in situations, such as public places, where the individual perceives the atmosphere to be dangerous.

Regardless of the fears you may have, the Bible tells us in 2 Timothy 1:7, *"For God gave us a spirit not of fear but of power and love and self-control."* If you really want to step into your calling and manifest your purpose, then you must choose not to allow fear to rule over you and to paralyze you. It is important for you to understand that:

Fear, worry, and anxiety are not from God. God has given you the power to overcome all of the negative forces coming against you!

The Bible says in Hebrews 11:27, it was by faith that Moses left Egypt. Let us think about this for a minute. Moses approached Pharaoh, the most powerful man in the world, and told him that he was taking his slave labor and leaving so that they could serve the God of Israel. Wow! Now, that is bold!

Do you want the same kind of boldness?

Are you ready to fulfill your destiny and take control of your own life?

You cannot let fear stop you from being who God destined you to be. When fear comes knocking at your door, you must answer it with faith. You must stay firmly rooted in Jesus and grounded in the truth of His words in order to be bold and courageous in the pursuit of your greatness. Remember, you are gifted. You are smart. God has qualified you. You can do it!

Cream and Sugar...

- *"Have I not commanded you? Be strong and courageous. Do not be frightened, and do not be dismayed, for the Lord your God is with you wherever you go."* **Joshua 1:9**
- *"I sought the Lord, and he answered me and delivered me from all my fears.***" Psalm 34:4**

Say this Prayer:

Dear Heavenly Father,

Today, I declare I will live by faith and not by fear. Help me not to be paralyzed by my fears, but when I am afraid, show me how to overcome anxiety, panic attacks, and worries.

Help me trust in You so I can rest in the confidence that You are with me. In Jesus' name, I pray, Amen.

Day 21

This Is the Right Time

He who observes the wind will not sow, and he who regards the clouds will not reap. ~Ecclesiastes 11:4

What are you waiting for? Are you waiting for a sign from God to chase your dreams? Maybe you are waiting to meet "Mr. Right" or for your child to go off to college. Are you waiting to have more money in your bank account? What excuses are causing you to delay pursuing your life's goals? Whatever your reasons are for waiting, stop it!

Stop it!

Stop it!

Stop it!

Stop waiting on perfect conditions to pursue your purpose and achieve your dreams.

I don't know about you, but I used to be the kind of person who needed everything to fall into place before I pursued my dreams, but the Holy Spirit taught me a valuable lesson. My avid pursuit for perfection fed into my habit of procrastination, which kept me from pursuing my goals.

Life is filled with uncertainty, responsibilities, pressures, and to-do-lists, and it is easy to feel both overwhelmed and underappreciated. I also recognize that there will be moments when the difficulties we face make us feel outmatched and "in way over our heads." Nevertheless, I would like to suggest that you are far more ready than you realize to pursue your goals. And if you will get in agreement with Jesus, you will start experiencing the greatest time of your life.

God is moving and He has so many incredible things that He wants to give to you and pour into your life. In fact, God will do amazing things in you and through you, so you can be blessed and become a blessing to other people. But you cannot wait for perfect conditions to chase your dreams, because you will never get started.

I want you to know that if you start where you are and with what you have, God in all of His greatness is able to take care of any lack you may have. It is important for you to know that:

When you are living by faith and not by sight, God will call you to move now and to have faith that your breakthrough is coming!

By the grace of God, you will accomplish things you have never been able to do in your past! Jesus is getting ready to place you in positions of influence, in strategic locations, with great purpose in mind, putting you on the path of success. Remember, all your help comes from the Lord! The time to get started is today! Your reward for starting today is the fulfillment of your God-given dream!

Cream and Sugar...

- *"For everything there is a season, and a time for every matter under heaven:"* **Ecclesiastes 3:1**
- *"Look carefully then how you walk, not as unwise but as wise, making the best use of the time, because the days are evil."* **Ephesians 5:15-16**

Say this prayer:

Dear Heavenly Father,

Today, remind me to follow Your lead. Help me to believe that Your timing is perfect, that You are always faithful. Give me the grace to be confident and competent in pursuing my dreams for Your glory. In Jesus' name, I pray, Amen.

Day 22

Watch Your Mouth!

Let the words of my mouth and the meditation of my heart be acceptable in your sight, O Lord, my rock and my redeemer. ~Psalms 19:14

"Watch your mouth!" is an expression I heard frequently from adults during my developmental years. However, did you know that the average person says around 16,000 words in a day? Wow! That is a lot of words to watch out for.

Sixteen thousand words give us many opportunities to empower and inspire someone. At the same time, there are several opportunities to stir up hatred and violence as well. In other words, we have plenty of chances to use our words for either good or evil.

Many times, we forget that words have real power. God spoke the world into existence by the authority of His words, and since we are created in His image, our words have power too. Nonetheless, from time to time, we say things without first thinking about them, and many of us pay the price for doing so. We need to understand that the words that we say out of our mouths do take on a life of their own.

Think about the words spoken to you by your parents, your friends, and your enemies. Did those words have an impact on your life?

God has given us many forewarnings throughout the Bible that tell us that our words play a very vital role in our lives. In the book of Proverbs, King Solomon wrote, *"Death and life are in the power of the tongue" (Proverbs 18:21).* Jesus declares in Matthew 12:37, *"for by your words you will be justified, and by your words you will be condemned."*

The Bible tells us that our tongue has the authority to direct where our life will take us.

> *"Look at the ships also: though they are so large and are driven by strong winds, they are guided by a very small rudder wherever the will of the pilot directs. So also the tongue is a small member, yet it boasts of great things." (James 3:4-5)*

If we lose control of our tongue and do not select our words wisely, our life is going to be impacted and taken off course, just as a ship is steered off course. In other words:

Your future is set in motion by your words, so affirm positive words to enrich your life positively.

No matter what is going on in your life today, it is time for you to "watch your mouth!" The next time you find yourself speaking words of disbelief and uncertainty, build yourself up by faith. Begin declaring God's truths over your life. Speak faith-filled words about your future because there is a miracle in your mouth. Stop talking about the problem and start talking about the solution. Start speaking words of victory not defeat!

P.S. Do not listen to negative people; instead, encourage yourself and speak LIFE over yourself!

Cream and Sugar...

- *"For "Whoever desires to love life and see good days, let him keep his tongue from evil and his lips from speaking deceit;"* **1 Peter 3:10**
- *"Do you see a man who is hasty in his words? There is more hope for a fool than for him."* **Proverbs 29:20**

Say this prayer:

Dear Heavenly Father:

Today I ask You to help me seek Your wisdom and words of healing when I am dealing with a problem. Guide me to make decisions and give guidance to others with words that edify, and words that honor You. In Jesus name, I pray, Amen.

Day 23

Your Inheritance Is Coming!

Whatever you do, work heartily, as for the Lord and not for men, knowing that from the Lord you will receive the inheritance as your reward. You are serving the Lord Christ. ~Colossians 3:23-24

The other night, I was watching *Brewster's Millions*, a 1985 comedy film starring Richard Pryor. Brewster was a minor-league baseball player and, unknown to him, he had a recently deceased rich relative. In order to test if Brewster knew the value of money, he was given the task of disposing of $30 million in 30 days. However, Brewster was not allowed to have any assets to show for the $30 million and was not allowed to waste the money in any way. If successful, Brewster would inherit $300 million.

Many of us secretly hope for that moment when we hear news of a great inheritance left to us by someone. The idea of getting something for nothing is powerful. Whether it is an inheritance, a lottery win, or some other windfall, the lure of fast money resulting in wealth and comfort can, at times, be very bewitching.

Do not get me wrong, it would be very nice to stumble across a treasure chest. However, unrealistic hopes often prove to be counterproductive, causing us to dream of something that **might** happen instead of planning for something that **will**. Rather than waiting for the pot of gold at the end of the rainbow, let us be productive and focused on where we are now and where we are going.

I have great news for you...there is an inheritance you already have! It is both surprising and overwhelming. It surprises us because it is something that we overlook and it is overwhelming because it completely rearranges our lives, our purpose, and our world-view.

This inheritance is our birthright. You do not have to work for it, earn it, or apply for it. This inheritance is passed down from the Father to his children, generation after generation. In fact, the Bible calls us heirs, which means we are the recipients of God's inheritance.

"In him we have obtained an inheritance, having been predestined according to the purpose of him who works all things according to the counsel of his will," (Ephesians 1:11)

Before we found ourselves in Christ, we were consumed by the fears and desires of a world that was blurred and at times twisted. Yet, as our lives are sown into His, we inherit qualities that empower us to rise above conditions, giving us clarity of understanding and a strengthened spirit we had not known before. If we are honest, we would admit that:

There was a time when we were ignorant of His nature, character and love, and still Jesus prepared this great inheritance for us.

As a child in God's family, you get to share in the family fortune; everything God has belongs to you. God has given you:

- The riches of His grace and mercy
- The riches of His kindness and glory
- The riches of His patience and wisdom
- The riches of His power and love

In addition to those wonderful riches, you will inherit eternal life in Heaven! How awesome is that?

You are far richer than you realize which is why the Apostle Paul could write with assurance, *"And my God will supply every need of yours according to his riches in glory in Christ Jesus" (Philippians 4:19)*. Your eternal inheritance is priceless, untainted, permanent, and secure; no one can take it from you.

There are so many days that come and go when we feel like we can't catch a break. It seems like everyone around us is being blessed and we are in the back, trying to find some reason to rejoice. However, let me tell you, in case you did not know this already, God's not finished with you yet!

So don't you dare give up because you are tired of waiting. God is not finished with you yet! The Lord hears your cries and your inheritance is on its way. Jesus is preparing something awesome for everything you have been through. Please continue to push forward, putting God first, and you will have it in a matter of time. It is written, *"What no eye has seen, nor ear heard, nor the heart of man imagined, what God has prepared for those who love Him." (1 Corinthians 2: 9)*

Cream and Sugar...

- *"A good man leaves an inheritance to his children's children, but the sinner's wealth is laid up for the righteous."* **Proverbs 13:22**
- *"The righteous shall inherit the land and dwell upon it forever."* **Psalm 37:29**

Say this prayer:

Dear Heavenly Father,

Today, I ask you to forgive me for living indigent instead of living like the child of the King that I am. Lord, help me remember the truth of who I am. Help me to take hold of Your precious promises and open my eyes to see what is important, which are the blessings You have given me. I pray that my life of suffering and lack will be replaced with ease, wealth, and abundance. In Jesus' name, I pray, Amen.

Day 24

Speak with Authority to Your Mountain!

He said to them, "Because of your little faith. For truly, I say to you, if you
have faith like a grain of mustard seed, you will say to this mountain,
'Move from here to there,' and it will move, and nothing will be impossible
for you." ~Matthew 17:20

What is a mountain? A mountain is anything that is a barrier to you completing the will of God. A mountain is anything that is impeding your progress to manifest your destiny. Sickness, despair, disruptive habits and financial difficulties are just a few examples of the mountains that some of us face every day.

What obstacles are you facing right now in your life? Are you in front of a massive mountain that seems too big to remove from your life? Are you going through a situation that has you feeling unsure of yourself? Is there something that seems to be standing in the way of your future, your success, and your purpose?

Jesus says in Mark 11:23, *"Truly, I say to you, whoever says to this mountain, 'Be taken up and thrown into the sea,' and does not doubt in his heart, but believes that what he says will come to pass, it will be done for him. Therefore, I tell you, whatever you ask in prayer, believe that you have received it, and it will be yours."*

That means we have to speak with authority and look at that mountain through our eyes of faith and say, "Mountain, you have to go! Flee from my life! Obstacles, you are subject to change! God is for me so who dare be against me?" However, do you know what happens most of the time? People end up talking **about** their mountains instead of talking **to** their mountains.

Jesus does not tell us to pray to the Father about these issues. He told His disciples to speak directly to the mountain and command it to be removed. Allow faith to arise in your heart and proclaim God's Word over your life no matter what you are facing. When you begin to speak to your mountain, when you speak with authority to your situations, something supernatural happens and that mountain has to move out of your way!

There are some storms we must go through and some we must speak to, but remember, God gave you the authority to move mountains!

One day, a co-worker of mine told me about his neighbor who was in excruciating pain from a stiff neck. Out of compassion for his neighbor, he and his wife decided to go to the neighbor's house, lay hands on him and pray for him.

They jumped into the car, drove over to his house and knocked on the door. When he answered, they said clearly and plainly, "We came here to pray for you." The neighbor was somewhat surprised, as he invited them in. Their prayer was simple and straight to the point, "In the Name of Jesus, I command this neck to be loosed and for all tight muscles to relax." They never prayed to the Father, they just spoke to the mountain. Within several minutes, the neighbor was completely healed.

Immediately after the neighbor realized what had happened, with tears running down his face, he asked them to pray for his sister-in-law, who was scheduled to see a doctor to remove cancer in her throat four days later. The husband turned to his wife and asked her to lay hands on the sister-in-law and pray.

She prayed the same prayer, "In the Name of Jesus, I command this cancer to die and to leave this body." Nothing visible happened at that moment but about a week later, they heard that when she went to the doctor for surgery the cancer was gone and there was no need for an operation!

This is not an isolated incident. All through the scriptures, the disciples used this principle to demonstrate the power of God. This same authority to work miracles through prayer has already been given to you by faith. You do not need a pastor, a bishop or some TV dude selling some special spring water. You already have this power to move any situation from your life, but you have to believe.

It is an unpleasant fact that all of us have mountains in our lives. However, God is a faithful God. All we have to do is follow His instructions and He will lead us to victory.

Cream and Sugar...

- *"The mountains melt like wax before the Lord, before the Lord of all the earth."* **Psalm 97:5**
- *"And this is the confidence that we have toward him, that if we ask anything according to his will he hears us."* **1 John 5:14**

Say this prayer:

Dear Heavenly Father,

Today I thank You for Your Word which is life to my spirit. I receive Your strength today and choose to speak to the mountains so I can move forward in the victory You have in store for me in Jesus' name, Amen.

Day 25

Great Relationships Equal Great Success

Therefore encourage one another and build one another up, just as you are doing. ~1 Thessalonians 5:11

Several years ago, I had the honor of speaking to a crowd of student-athletes in Washington, DC. It was a wonderful feeling to be able to go back to the environment that had a major impact on the person I have become today. It was great to be a voice to the future young minds of tomorrow.

Shortly after I finished speaking, I did an interview with one of the local newspaper reporters. During the interview, the reporter asked specifically about what I would say to the youth in light of these uncertain financial times and the political climate. My answer to him is what I want to share with you today, with the hope that it will enlighten you.

When stuff appears complicated and doubtful, we have to put a spotlight on what is certain in our lives: our friends, our families, and most importantly, our relationship with Jesus Christ. We always have to remind ourselves to find balance in our day-to-day living, even when the world around us seems unstable.

Think about that person that loves to go rock climbing up a mountain. In the movies, there is always a person at the top of the mountain reaching their hand down to help someone else to get to the top. You always hear the same phrase, "don't look down" and the next thing that person does, is look down and lose focus on the individual trying to help him or her reach the top of the mountain.

Unfortunately, we have all been in a position where we've felt like we were climbing that massive mountain. When our foot starts to slip, that is when we should reach up and grab hold of our relationships. We have to reach for those individuals that have supported us in the past; our relationships are our support system. It is why one of the most important decisions we make in life is whom we choose to be around.

And it's extremely important for you to know that:

Great relationships begin on spiritual and intellectual levels: levels of prayer, purpose, passion, and personality.

It is painful when you realize you were more invested in a friendship than the other person. Nevertheless, do not withdraw from everyone because a positive support system will assist you in accomplishing the task at hand.

115

Being in a circle of great relationships will provide the necessary tools to help you climb any mountain that you may ever face. You can have all the money in the world, but if you do not have a support system, if you are not connected with people in healthy ways, then you will not fulfill your destiny nor be able to live the way God intended.

The Bible says in Proverbs 27: 9, *"The heartfelt counsel of a friend is as sweet as perfume and incense."* Our ability to build and maintain healthy relationships is the single most important factor that determines how we get along in every area of life. Therefore, I encourage you today to treasure the people in your life. Be willing to make adjustments and modifications to improve your relationships.

It is one thing to say you are a friend and an entirely different thing to actually be a friend! One-way friendships, partnerships and relationships will ultimately lead to a dead end. Without dependable and trustworthy reciprocity, we find ourselves alone.

If you want to continue to move forward in the right direction in life, remember, people are God's priority, and when you make the people in your life your priority, you are taking steps towards building great success. All of life's successes come from initiating relationships with the right

116

people, then strengthening those relationships by using the love of God.

Cream and Sugar...

- *"Greater love has no one than this, that someone lay down his life for his friends."* **John 15:13**
- *"Iron sharpens iron, and one man sharpens another."* **Proverbs 27:17**

Say this Prayer:

Dear Heavenly Father,

Today, please have mercy on me. You know my shortcomings and difficulties, so I'm asking You to strengthen and heal my relationships. I am weak, but You are the Divine Healer and strengthener of my heart and soul. Guide me to do Your will in this world, to love and respect others, and to be Your representative among my relationships. In Jesus' name, I pray, Amen.

Day 26

Don't Settle for Less

For I know the plans I have for you, declares the Lord, plans for welfare and not for evil, to give you a future and a hope.~ Jeremiah 29:11

Have you ever seen the movie called, *City of Angels*?

It is a 1998 romantic fantasy film starring Nicolas Cage and Meg Ryan. *City of Angels* tells the story of an angel named Seth (Cage) who watches over humans and protects them in undetected ways. Seth's main duty is to appear to those who are near death and lead them to the next life. During the story, Seth falls in love with a woman (Ryan) and gives up his angelic status to become human in order to be with her.

Now, I will not lie to you, I thought it was a good movie. However, I started wondering, why would an angel consider giving up the best relationship, with God, to settle for a human relationship? Then, I realized we all have settled for less at some point in our lives.

Adam and Eve had the perfect relationship with God in the Garden of Eden, but they settled for less by eating from the forbidden tree. Judas was in the perfect position for greatness, but he settled for less by betraying Jesus for thirty pieces of silver. As for me, there have been times I have settled for less by focusing on worldly things rather than the Word of God.

Over the last 10 years, I noticed that very few are committed to God's best. All too often, individuals respond to their future by simply settling into boring, mediocre lives. However, that is not the type of life God wants for anyone!

We have been conditioned by the world to "dumb down" and accept far less than what God has provided. As a matter of fact, the only reason we are not receiving God's best is because we are willing, consciously or unconsciously, to settle for less.

Here are five warning signs that you are settling for less:

1. You blame other people.

2. You think a lot, but do very little.

3. You are continuously jealous.

4. Food, alcohol, or TV are the highlight of your day.

5. You do not think you can.

Listen, you are the child of the Most High God. You are a citizen of the Kingdom of Heaven, which means you have far-reaching influence, access to unlimited resources, and endless opportunities. Seize the opportunities!

The minute you settle for less than you deserve, is the same minute you settle for less than what God created you for.

It is time for you to put your faith in God's power and take advantage of the opportunities He gives you. If you refuse to settle for a life of mediocrity, you will be able to pursue the excellence God has in store for you. You will be able to fulfill your greatest potential. You will live fearlessly in the face of difficulty.

So, get out of your comfort zone and take the risks God calls you to take. Be on the lookout for divine appointments because He is getting ready to promote you. Ask God to give you the wisdom to do the right thing, for the right reason, in the right way, at the right time. Remember, God is faithful to keep all of His promises and He has far more for you than what you are experiencing.

Set your mind on the things of God and not on the things of this world. Jesus has paid a way for you to be free from the strongholds of mediocrity. He stands ready to lead you to His perfect plan for your life. For that reason, stop

120

putting limitations on your thinking. God did not create you to be average. You were created to shine. Keep pursuing God's very best for you!

Cream and Sugar...

- *"Oh, taste and see that the Lord is good! Blessed is the man who takes refuge in him!"* **Psalm 34:8**
- *"Let us know; let us press on to know the Lord; his going out is sure as the dawn, he will come to us as the showers, as the spring rains that water the earth."* **Hosea 6:3**

Say this prayer:

Dear Heavenly Father,

Today, I am reminded that I am Your child and a citizen of Your Kingdom. Help me be faithful to live a life beyond my limitations according to Your plan and purpose for me. I will center my life on You rather than myself. I pray this in Jesus' name, Amen.

Day 27

Decide To Love Since God's Love Never Fails

Let all that you do be done in love. ~1 Corinthians 16:14

Similar to prayer, I know there is no way I can write what I want to say about love in a few pages. To be honest, the richness and depth of love is more than a decision. Nevertheless, for the sake of today's devotional, I will try to help you understand the significance of deciding to love.

Sooner or later, life will turn every individual upside down and topsy-turvy. However, one mishap, misstep, or mistake does not define an individual. Even though we make mistakes and fail, God's love never fails. Absolutely nothing can separate us from the love of God: not death nor life, neither a messenger of Heaven nor a ruler of earth, not what happens today nor what may happen tomorrow, neither a power from on high nor a power from below, neither the thinkable nor unthinkable.

God's love for us stands forever and that is just one reason, out of hundreds of reasons, why we must decide to love God and others with everything we have, with every fiber of our being.

Love is the foundation upon which everything else is established. Love is more than impulses, feelings, or passing desires. Love is the one virtue that ties everything together in unity. Love demands us to be kind and patient. Love demands a sacrifice. Love is a commitment.

Love is greater than faith and hope. Love is an unshakable intention, regardless of the cost. Truthfully, the only reason we can love God or anybody else is because God first loved us. He showed this love by creating us. Our Heavenly Father showed His love by sending Jesus Christ to earth to die for us. Therefore, love is putting another person's interests ahead of our own.

"A new commandment I give to you, that you love one another: just as I have loved you, you also are to love one another."(John13:34)

Love is of God and God is love. As a matter of fact, everything God does is impelled and influenced by His love. His love surpasses all human knowledge, and it is challenging for any of us to grasp the width, length, height, and depth of God's love. It is important for you to know that:

Jesus does not love you because of your character; He loves you because of His perfect character.

Jesus longs to have a loving relationship with you. His love goes beyond any human love you have ever experienced. If you decide to lean into the unconditional, unfailing, unbreakable love of Jesus Christ, your love will become patient and generous, just and forgiving. You will be able to overcome any betrayal, hurt, or crushing defeat. You will have an influence far greater than you could ever envision.

I would like you to spend the next few minutes reflecting on the role of love in your love life.

Whom do you have a difficult time loving?

_____

_____

_____

_____

_____

_____

What can you do to demonstrate the love of Jesus Christ?

_____

_____

_____

_____

_____

Cream and Sugar...

- *"Love is patient and kind; love does not envy or boast; it is not arrogant or rude. It does not insist on its own way; it is not irritable or resentful; it does not rejoice at wrongdoing, but rejoices with the truth. Love bears all things, believes all things, hopes all things, endures all things. Love never ends."* **1 Corinthians 13:4-8**

- *"And above all these put on love, which binds everything together in perfect harmony."* **Colossians 3:14**

Say this Prayer:

Dear Heavenly Father,

Today, I want to thank You that You are a loving, gracious God. Thank You that Your love is perfect, it never fails, and that nothing can separate me from Your love. Help me to love as You love. Fill me with Your Spirit so that I can choose what is best because I don't want to settle for less. In Jesus' name, I pray, Amen.

Day 28

From Dreams to Action

So also faith by itself, if it does not have works, is dead. ~James 2:17

I have always had a shy personality. Psychologists would label me as having an introverted temperament which means:

- I have an attitude that is reserved, quiet, and questioning.
- I like to think and process inwardly before giving an answer.
- I tend to speak slower, and I like to state my thoughts without interruption.
- I need less verbal feedback and affirmation from others.
- I have many conversations within my own mind every day.
- I like to forethink, reflect, and then act.

Basically, I am a dreamer with a vivid imagination, a homebody who loves to get lost in the world of ideas rather than in the world of things. Despite the fact that I am an introvert, I always felt like there was something great on the inside of me trying to get out.

When I was in the eighth-grade, a few of my neighborhood friends and I started an R&B singing group. Our first (and last) performance was at our middle school's spring talent show. Naturally, I was extremely nervous, to the point that I could feel my pulse pounding in my temples. To make matters worse, I was going through puberty; my voice was changing. But nothing was going to stop me, because I had dreams of being the next singing sensation and I wanted all the girls to like me.

To make a long story short, I was horrible! Awful! Dreadful! I completely embarrassed myself. My voice was flat, raspy, and weak. Did I mention that I forgot my lines? I am so glad people did not have smart phones back then; it would have gone viral.

As I reflect on that horrific experience, I am so glad God allowed me to go through it. My dreadful performance helped me develop a resilient character. It was my first lesson in putting action behind my dreams.

Today, I want you to put action behind your dreams. Put action behind your faith and make the most of every opportunity God gives you. Leave no opportunity unexplored or unknown!

Pursuing your dreams is an important part of manifesting your destiny; therefore, never use the excuse that it's too late. JESUS has risen, which means He can resurrect your lost dreams, broken relationships, and restore every area of your life!

If you really want amazing things to happen in your life, you will have to prepare. Success happens when preparation meets opportunity. I like to say it this way:

Prior preparation prevents poor performance.

It is important to use and develop the gifts God has given you so when an opportunity presents itself, you are able to walk through that open door with boldness and confidence.

So, keep the fire in your heart alive. Stay true to your beliefs. Do not worry about embarrassing yourself. Every day you are one day closer to achieving your dreams.

Start using what you have and doing what you know to do, and God will open the door to new opportunities. Remember, life is lived one day at a time, and the way to prepare for tomorrow is to live at your very best today.

Cream and Sugar...

- *"As each has received a gift, use it to serve one another, as good stewards of God's varied grace:"* **1 Peter 4:10**

- *"Now to him who is able to do far more abundantly than all that we ask or think, according to the power at work within us"* **Ephesians 3:20**

Say this Prayer:

Dear Heavenly Father,

Today, remind me to follow Your lead. Help me to believe that Your timing is perfect, that You are always faithful. Give me the grace to be confident and competent in pursuing my dreams for Your glory. In Jesus' name, I pray, Amen.

Day 29

Breaking the Strongholds

For though we walk in the flesh, we are not waging war according to the flesh. For the weapons of our warfare are not of the flesh but have divine power to destroy strongholds. ~ *2 Corinthians 10:3-4*

Do you feel nothing but despair?

Do you think thoughts of defeat?

Do you wonder why you keep struggling and stumbling with the same weakness, hardship, or sin?

Do strongholds have a strong hold on you?

The Bible tells us that the enemy (Satan), who the Bible describes as a thief, comes to steal, kill and destroy. He wants us to live our lives in defeat, and one of the ways he does this is through strongholds. These strongholds can affect our attitudes, emotional state, and our reactions to different situations. They influence our spiritual liberty.

A stronghold is a false principle or idea that rejects God's truth and promises. According to 2 Corinthians 10:5, strongholds are disdainful opinions raised against the knowledge of God, and takes every thought to obey Christ captive. In other words, strongholds attempt to magnify the problem and minimize God's ability to solve it.

To help you understand a little more, here are few examples:

- God will never forgive me. - The stronghold of guiltiness
- Bad things always happen to me. - The stronghold of depression
- I am far too good to have to put up with this. - The stronghold of pride
- I am not worthy of love. - The stronghold of rejection

Most Christians are not aware of strongholds in their lives, but you do not have to be among them. You have the divine authority to demolish any stronghold that is keeping you from God's blessings, that is keeping you from experiencing spiritual freedom through Christ. Remember, you are a victor through Jesus Christ.

Everything that we see is a shadow cast by that which we do not see. God made us conquerors; therefore, we will be victorious!

Are you ready to break the strongholds in your life? You must start by being transformed by the renewing of your mind!

"Do not be conformed to this world, but be transformed by the renewal of your mind, that by testing you may discern what is the will of God, what is good and acceptable and perfect." (Romans 12:2)

As you renew your mind daily through the Word of God and prayer, your thoughts are transformed and strongholds are torn down; false thinking patterns are corrected with the truth. Nonetheless, I would like to give you two tips to help keep the strongholds broken.

1. **Submit to God in humility.** Humility is one of the best weapons against pride. When pride is removed, strongholds are weakened. *"But he gives more grace. Therefore it says, "God opposes the proud but gives grace to the humble." Submit yourselves therefore to God. Resist the devil, and he will flee from you." (James 4:6-7)*

2. **Exchange every lie with God's truth**. For example, if the lie is "I am a failure, I can do nothing right"— memorize Philippians 4:13, *"I can do all things through Christ which strengthens me."* The more verses you

have committed to memory the stronger you will be when the enemy attacks your mind with negative thoughts.

Now you know the truth! Begin today to fill your mind with the amazing and loving thoughts of God. Start feeding your soul with God's truths. Your health, your peace, and your prosperity will go to another level when those strongholds are destroyed.

Visualize faith rising in your heart and declare what God says about your future. Be determined that you will not be denied. Now, arise precious child of God, and go have a great day!

Cream and Sugar...

- *"For we do not wrestle against flesh and blood, but against the rulers, against the authorities, against the cosmic powers over this present darkness, against the spiritual forces of evil in the heavenly places."* **Ephesians 6:12**
- *"The Lord is my light and my salvation; whom shall I fear? The Lord is the stronghold of my life; of whom shall I be afraid?"* **Psalm 27:1**

Say this Prayer:

Dear Heavenly Father,

Today, help me to begin to be more spiritually aware of the potential strongholds in my life. I declare, in the name of Jesus, that any stronghold of fear, doubt, shame, or unbelief be broken. And I claim freedom in Jesus Christ. I pray this in Jesus' name, Amen.

Day 30

Realizing the High Aspiration

Delight yourself also in the Lord, and He will give you the desires and of your heart. ~Psalm 37:4

James Allen once said, "You will become as small as your controlling desire; as great as your dominant aspiration."

What does that mean to you? I have a better question: what is your aspiration?

The definition of aspiration is the desire or ambition to achieve something. Now, I know that is a very simple definition; however, aspirations produce the thought-provoking life people seek by helping them concentrate on motivating and exhilarating life goals. Aspirations can be the driving force in someone's life and allow him or her to feel like they are on top of the world.

If we are honest with ourselves, motivation to achieve or to become successful is very vital to our human needs. Without it, to a certain degree, we never become our maximum selves. However, did you know that it is through our desires and attainment of our desires that we develop and grow – not through the result of our desires?

Let me explain:

There's nothing quite like stepping into something new.

- New clothes.

- A new car.

- A new house.

- A new job.

- A new relationship.

Nevertheless, have you ever noticed that when we get that new thing, we constantly want something that is newer? We always have greater and greater desires.

As Christians, we have the custom of praying and wanting the next best thing. As soon as we achieve or attain a specific object, we eventually want to get a newer model, an upgrade. For example, you may work extremely hard to buy yourself the new iPhone, a new car, a new house, but at some point, you quickly feel like it is not enough and you want a newer iPhone, newer car, a bigger house.

Even though, there is nothing wrong with what you currently have, your desire for that particular phone, car, or house is gone. A level of emptiness emerges, and at that moment, you start looking for ways to replace what you have with something newer.

(Side Note: I find it interesting that many individuals have this same approach with their relationships and their marriages.)

But, that's a huge mistake!

Our focus should not be on replacing the items; we should focus on replacing the desire by cultivating an even more challenging desire. We need to start praying and looking for the next challenge, because it is in the challenge that you will find satisfaction for your desire. Do you see the difference? In other words, the object will never satisfy you, the challenge to attain the object will. Keep this in mind:

Do not look at what you already achieved, but look at what you aspire to achieve.

God will use challenges to help you reach your desires, to help you manifest your destiny, which will develop your character. Nevertheless, I have to make sure I say this: it is all for God's glory. Therefore, as you pursue your aspirations for life, remember God created us for his glory and your aspirations should be for His glory as well.

I want you to understand that there is nothing wrong with pursuing the desires of your heart. Besides, God wants to give you the desires of your heart, if you delight yourself in Him. It is important for you to have a balanced approach to pursuing those desires, which includes setting goals by prayer, wisdom, and humility. Use preparation and dedication to drive yourself towards God-given aspirations and make sure to praise His name during the process.

Cream and Sugar...

- *"What the wicked dreads will come upon him, but the desire of the righteous will be granted."* **Proverbs 10:24**
- *"The plans of the heart belongs to man, but the answer of the tongue is from the Lord. All the ways of a man are pure in his own eyes, but the Lord weighs the spirit. Commit your work to the Lord, and your plans will be established."* **Proverbs 16:1-3**

Say this Prayer:

Dear Heavenly Father,

Today, I pray that the dreams and ambitions You placed within my heart are fulfilled according to Your will and purpose for my life. My deepest satisfaction comes from glorifying Your great name through my desires. In Jesus' name, I pray, Amen.

My Open Letter to You!

Dear Friend,

I write this letter to you with a joyous heart, with the hope that your experiences with God are as life-changing as mine. I speak grace and peace to you many times over, as you deepen your love with God through Jesus Christ, our Lord.

What a mighty God we have! And how fortunate we are to have Him, this Father of our Lord Jesus! Because Jesus was raised from the dead, we've been given a brand-new life and have everything to live for, including a future in heaven! To Him is the glory both now and forever!

I know how great this must make you feel, because you have never seen Him, yet, you love Him. You still don't see Him, yet, you trust him. Therefore, because you keep believing in the Son of God, I pray that God bless you with everything that is good and wonderful according to His will.

I know you have traveled far down the road of life and enjoyed many favors and wonderful blessings. However, what are your expectations?

I want to challenge your expectations for your future because I have learned over the last 20 years that expectations can be high or low, rational or irrational, noble or ruthless. Nevertheless, I truly believe in the importance of high expectations for yourself as an individual and for the life you plan to live.

The devil is going to try to influence and impact your future by getting you to expect the worst! If you do, he will provide you with the right conditions, signs and sentiments to confirm your worst fears. However, if you take hold of God's Word and raise your expectations, you will start to see God move in a mighty way, making the impossible possible.

Here is my last quote until I write to you again:

Great accomplishments will continuously be present in the framework of great expectations.

Always remember, living forward is having the expectation that no matter what happens, God is ordering your steps. Your expectation will cause you to be at the right place at the right time, not only for your good and the good of others, but for the glory of our Heavenly Father.

Never lower your expectations to meet your performance or skill level. Raise your level of performance to meet your expectations. Expect the best for your future because Jesus wants to use you to fulfill His plan on the earth.

Wake up every day with an open heart, ready to be used by God for His glory. Let Him be Lord over everything in your life because He can change any situation. And I will leave you with this: instead of getting worked up and frustrated about things that happened yesterday, trust God and know that today is a gift, so you can start living your best life forward with a little bit of coffee and a whole a lot of Jesus.

Your Brother-in-Christ,

Tony Warrick

Tony L. Warrick

CAN YOU DO ME A FAVOR?

First, if you enjoyed Jesus and Coffee, would you take a few moments and write a review on Amazon? A short review will help, and it would mean a lot to me. Leave a short review at http://bit.ly/JesusandCoffeeBook

Secondly, if you know someone who needs to be encouraged, inspired, and motivated, please send him or her a copy of this book.

Thirdly, do not forget to join my Dream Team! The Dream Team members are the first to know about new book releases, videos and special offers and have access to exclusive content. Additionally, you will have the chance to win a few prizes such as:

- An autographed copy of my books
- An opportunity to win a $25 Visa gift card
- An opportunity to win a free vacation for two

Join the Dream Team by going to http://bit.ly/DreamTeamNow

Lastly, if you have not downloaded my free eBook, you can download it at http://bit.ly/DecideEbook

Thank you so much for reading Jesus and Coffee. Now, go enlarge your vision with a little bit of coffee and a lot of Jesus!

Acknowledgements

A special thanks to my precious wife (Ashley) who has loved me and encouraged me throughout this process. I am grateful for the support I have received during the development of this book. You have touched and marked my life far beyond words.

A special shout out to Derron E. Short, my gifted and diligent advisor, who helped me shape this book from its early formless stage to its present form.

A special appreciation to my social media family who journeyed with me on my social media adventure. Thank you for motivating me to keep writing and following Jesus passionately into my destiny.

About the Author

Dr. Tony L. Warrick has always had a passion for transformation. This passion unveiled his purpose to see people be all that God has created them to be by connecting the transforming power of Jesus Christ to everyday living.

Born and raised in Washington, D.C., Dr. Warrick overcame incredible odds from his youth by pulling from the grace he experienced during his darkest lessons to help individuals change their lives, through spiritual health, personal growth, and professional development. His writings provide daily action steps for every area of a Christian life. It is his aspiration that people are equipped with practical principles to navigate the complex challenges life can bring, while moving forward and making a huge impact in their community.

To learn more about Dr. Warrick, please visit:

TonyWarrick.com

twitter.com/IamTonyWarrick

facebook.com/IamTonyWarrick

Made in the USA
Columbia, SC
11 March 2018